# SO, YOU WANT TO BE A
# LANDLORD, EH?

### A Memoir

*A humorous,
and sometimes harrowing,
tale of the trials
and tribulations
of being a landlord*

## Kevin Clarke

So, You Want to be a Landlord, eh?
Copyright © 2020 by Kevin Clarke

All rights reserved. No part of this publication may be reproduced, distributed, or transmitted in any form or by any means, including photocopying, recording, or other electronic or mechanical methods, without the prior written permission of the author, except in the case of brief quotations embodied in critical reviews and certain other non-commercial uses permitted by copyright law.

Tellwell Talent
www.tellwell.ca

ISBN
978-0-2288-4169-2 (Paperback)

**For mom and dad**

# FOREWORD

Over the last few years my mother has said that I should write a memoir. I thought it was a neat idea, but also a daunting task. First of all, where would I start? At my first memory? If so, then what would that be? At this point in my life, can I even remember what it was? What's my problem with that? My mother is 95 years old now and told me recently her first memory was from when she was 4 or 5 years old! Oh-oh, I'm only 64!

I thought about it, writing a memoir, and decided that since I'm retired and have a bit of time on my hands, I'd give it a go. I thought, look, everybody has a story, several of them in fact. But sixty-four years seemed like a long time with a lot of things that had happened, so I needed to simplify it. I reflected on my life and it seems to have been in stages:

Childhood – carefree
Young adulthood – independence
Adulthood – responsibilities
Mid-life – building wealth
Retirement – volunteering

Through every one of those stages there was a common theme. Be the person my parents taught me to be: respectful, work hard, do my best, and have fun. I've tried my best to do all those things and, by-and-large, I believe I've been able to. Alas, such is life, I know I have not succeeded in every instance.

Given that this was prompted by my mother's encouragement, and in the true spirit of her never-ending search for a laugh, I thought it would be easier for me, and funnier for her, to capture one stage of my life - my time as a landlord. They definitely were not all funny times, as you will find out, but they sure seem like it now. It might not be exactly what she had in mind, which probably would not surprise her, but she definitely influenced my telling of the story.

# AUTHOR'S NOTE

He was a bear of a man – looked like one (pushing six-feet tall and a hearty 385 pounds), walked like one, was as hairy as one, and growled like one. He was the superintendent on one of our construction jobs in small town Alberta. His favourite expression whenever someone did something wrong or stupid was always difficult to make out. He had a way of speaking the words that left an uncertainty in your mind, "That was stupid, *Ethel*", or "Why did you do that, *Ethel*?" All of us on the crew swore that he was saying "*Asshole*" and not "*Ethel*", but we were not quite sure.

# PART 1
# WHY DO THIS THING?

## *The Germ Takes Root*

After I hitchhiked out west in the mid-seventies, like all my buddies were doing, I ended up working for a big company for ten years in Alberta. The dream job where I got my Journeyman ticket. Set for life with the sweet pension at the end. Living in the land of milk and honey in those days was great, except maybe for the long, cold winters. Sometimes it got to 40 below zero and regularly to 25 below, and my job was mostly outdoors.

I remember taking a night course on personal finances, how to save and invest money in different ways. A lot of it focused on how to secure a decent retirement and how much money you would need to do that. At that time, I was looking at having a fully funded pension plan when I was 65 years old, maybe even retire at sixty. That sure looked good, but it also looked like a long time away, since I was only in my mid-20s at the time.

I learned a lot about the financial markets, like the features of common and preferred shares, interest bearing and strip bonds, the effects of inflation, selling short and long, etc. Many of the people in the class, I imagined, were not working in big companies with the fat pension plan to rely on in their retirement. Even though I was in a good position pension-wise, the professor said one thing that stuck with me – "You need to find a way to *create wealth*. That would come in perilously handy later.

It turned out that I left that company after ten years and moved about four-thousand kilometers back to the Maritimes where I grew up. Goodbye pension. Goodbye minus 40!

## _The Infection Festers_

The funny thing is that it started out simply enough, this whole idea of buying a small apartment building in the hope of *building equity* and *becoming rich*. It turns out that the only thing I became rich in was stories about the people I met along the way. I ended up with three buildings that contained a total of eight apartment units. I can't count the number of tenants that rented from me over some twenty-odd years, but I remember a great many of them.

The key problem for me with becoming a landlord was that I never really had the type of personality to be one in the first place. Self-reflection for me was a Monday morning quarterback kind of thing. I never assessed beforehand the potential problems and challenges of owning a rental property or read anything that warned of the financial pitfalls and stress that being a landlord might create.

Personality-wise I tend to sympathize with people and their difficult situations. My problem was that mostly I took the same approach to people in my business relationships (tenants) as I did in my personal relationships. Of course what I should have done was establish some distance with my tenants and learn to empathize with them, rather than sympathise with them. I also should have held firm positions with them on where the line in the sand really was.

To be fair to myself though, there is very little support from the Residential Tenancies Board for landlords, so it makes it pretty difficult to take any firm, or what most people would consider reasonable, actions outside the rigid framework of The Act. Maybe that's why everybody called it the "Tenant" Board. Now I always laugh when I hear people talk about how powerful landlords are, and I've heard it a lot, when in fact the regulations are all in favour of the tenants (more on that later).

So, here's another problem. I'm a rule follower. I get my vehicle inspection stickers, licence plates, and driver's licence renewed on time. I'm at appointments ten minutes beforehand. I pay my bills ahead of time, and if one seems to be lower than what I believed was the correct amount, I'll even ask to see if it's correct. It goes on and on.

I'm a reader of regulations too, which is also the type of thing I did for a living in my job as a safety officer. I prefer to know not what I can get away with, but what I'm allowed to do. There's a much different way of thinking between those two things. I've always had a fairly positive outlook on life in most situations, meaning that I believe people will be reasonable and try to work things out on a win-win basis. HA! I still choose to be positive, but I've come to learn that things *do not* work that way. When the chips are down, people will do what's in their best interest. It's only natural, nothing personal, right? So, given my way of thinking, I'm really the author of any misfortune that has befallen me.

My neighbourhood was close to the "old bridge" in Dartmouth, Nova Scotia, just a ten-minute drive to downtown Halifax. What do they always say – LOCATION, LOCATION, LOCATION! My house was also next to a full city block park that had seen better days. So too had the neighbourhood.

There were no families with young children left to occupy the mostly wonderful old homes in the neighbourhood, many of which survived the Halifax Explosion of 1917. Let's face it, a lot of the houses were fairly run down. A few were boarding houses and low-rise apartment walk-ups in which you really didn't want to imagine what was going on. The volume of the music, the arguments, and the roaring vehicles told the tale.

I got to know a couple of my very nice neighbours and of course you know where the conversations always went. Life is funny sometimes. Shortly after moving in I noticed a guy across the street from my house a few times who looked kind of familiar and he kept going in and out of his big garage. One day I spied an old Norton motorcycle in the garage, so I went over to say hello and introduce myself. When he told me his name I was taken aback. It turned out that he had a band years ago that we used to hire now and again for our community centre dances in New Brunswick. Well, I was only about 14 or 15-years old back then, so it was quite a surprise to meet up with a musician who I'd basically worshipped.

It was the early 70s then and he was the singer/guitarist who played songs like "I Heard It Through the Grapevine" and "Tobacco Road". He was like our Otis Redding or Marvin Gaye with the big afro and a captivating, to say the least, stage presence. They were always the best band to hire and since they came from the (then) mysterious province of Nova Scotia, they were a really big draw and played all of the best current hits. I never talked to him much about his band-playing days, but they must have been wild times. These days he was a regular work-a-day guy who was a born-again Christian. He ended up being a big influencer in the eventual turn-around of our neighbourhood.

# PART 2
# INTO THE ABYSS

# CHAPTER 1

# Johnny's Place

I had owned my house in Dartmouth for about five years. There was a house down the adjacent street that was an old two-bedroom, two-storey built in the early 1900s. It had been converted into a triplex building with a self-contained bachelor apartment added on the ground level at the back, and a self-contained one-bedroom apartment above it on the second story. The house was on the largest lot on the street and had a long gravel driveway that led to an old broken-down garage. It faced the park and had a nice view of the MacDonald Bridge lit up at night.

The house had been a problem for years and was a topic of discussion at every chat I had with my neighbours. There were always rough looking guys hanging around drinking beer and smoking God knows what. I noticed that the cars around there, on any given day, had different licence plates on them than the day before. I still don't know what that was all about, but I'm sure it wasn't good. This house and a couple of others around the park were rented out to heavy drinkers, drug users, dealers and prostitutes.

So, we got a community group started with some of the younger people who had moved into the area. As more of the residents joined the group, we began to invite the police and city council members to our meetings hoping for feedback and solutions to our concerns. The advice we were given was to *call, call, call* the police at every opportunity.

There was one car from another property down the block that had the loudest and most annoying muffler you ever heard. He was constantly peeling around the neighbourhood, probably on his illicit drug delivery runs, and it absolutely drove "Otis" crazy. He always led off our community meetings with a prayer, and he was as inspirational at that as he was when he sang "Foxy Lady" back in the day. He was still rockin' alright, but rollin' to a higher power this time.

People around the park had begun to fix up their properties, and the city started to make improvements to the park. One day I was up working on the roof of my house when I saw smoke coming out of an upstairs window of the house two doors down the street. It was a boarding house and one of the problems in the neighbourhood. The first thing I thought was, GREAT! Burn the place down! Then I thought the reasonable thing, "Good Lord, there could be people in there." I called the fire department and they put out the fire. The property sold after that and the family who moved in started to fix it up.

Everyone hoped that the triplex down the street would be fixed up and one day it went up for sale. Since

I had some equity available, I decided to take a look at it. Boy, was that scary!

The bank had repossessed the house and put it on the market. The house was vacant, and all the windows were boarded up. All the exterior doors were solid metal with no windows. The property was a real blight on the neighbourhood.

The two-bedroom, two-storey unit had not been upgraded in decades. There was a fabulous south-facing sun porch on the front that had windows so old you could see the ripples in the glass from all the years of summer heat. Surprisingly none of them were broken. There was a fireplace in the living room with hardwood floors in both the living room and dining room, which was standard for those houses. They definitely needed refinishing, but it was a nice feature. Just about everything else was a problem, the walls and ceilings were damaged, all the cast iron radiators were gone, the windows had mold on their wooden frames, light fixtures were broken or missing, you name it – it was wrecked.

The only thing that seemed to survive the destruction was the nice banister and staircase to the upper floor. There were dead and decaying birds on the floor in the master bedroom and several pellet holes in the walls. The basement had its own problems. It had flooded and the boiler and electric water heaters (one for each unit) were beyond repair. The roof was in such bad condition that it needed to be stripped and re-roofed. The vinyl siding wasn't too bad except for a bit of graffiti sprayed on a small area near the back. The chimney was in good condition, but the fireplace couldn't be used due to the lack of a chimney-liner. That didn't need to be installed because I figured you probably didn't want tenants to have open flames in their apartment. If only I had been that wise and forward thinking in some of the other decisions that I made about tenant behaviour!

After having seen the 2-bedroom unit, the bachelor apartment didn't seem too bad, mostly because it was so small. I guess there's only so much damage you can do to a four-hundred square-foot apartment. Still in all, just like the other apartment, the fridge and stove had to go, and the floors and windows needed some serious repairs. The bathroom was absolutely disgusting with broken and missing wall tiles and heavy mold everywhere.

I went up to the one-bedroom apartment via the rotting exterior staircase. It had a big deck that ran across the length of the back of the apartment, about twenty-two feet long. There was a nice view of the back lawn and heavily treed back yard, apparently a drug dealers paradise – very secluded! It was quite a shock when the agent opened the door to go in. Every surface: walls, ceilings, baseboards, door trim, and cupboards, was *painted black!* Even in the bathroom. I can't imagine what kind of scary dude lived there, but thankfully he's not someone who appears in my story!

The rest of the apartment was in the same condition as the other two units, seriously damaged. It was a nice layout though for 450sq. feet. Upon entering on the left side of the deck there was a small coat closet and then running to the back on that side was the fridge, which of course wasn't there, then the counter and sink, and then the stove. The kitchen area was big enough for a kitchen table and three chairs. Behind the wall by the stove was a small bathroom with a sink/vanity, toilet and tub/shower. To the right of the entrance was a half-wall separating the kitchen area from the living room. The small bedroom and closet were at the back righthand side of the apartment.

So, there it was. A wreck of a building that had tons of potential. A "diamond in the rough", possibly! The neighbourhood had suffered some serious decline over probably the last twenty years as families had aged and all the kids moved out. Now there were younger people moving back in and rejuvenating their properties and the neighbourhood. The location was definitely good, exceptionally good in fact. Basically, ten to fifteen minutes driving from almost anywhere you would be working in the Halifax/Dartmouth area. The main Dartmouth bus terminal was only a two-minute walk away, perfect for renters with no vehicle.

The repairs and renovations that were required included a new roof, new decks and exterior stairs, new windows, new exterior doors (with windows!), removal of the garage (which I'll get to later), a paved driveway and parking area out back. The hardwood floors needed to be refinished, walls and ceilings needed to be repaired and painted in all three units, and all the appliances had to be installed. The boiler and radiators for heating in the two-bedroom apartment had to be purchased and installed, along with the three electric hot water tanks in the basement. The electric radiators for the bachelor and one-bedroom apartments needed to be changed out. The wiring had been upgraded when the apartments out back were added to the building, so there was no problem with that, and each unit had its own electrical panel. The main plumbing system appeared to be okay (I'll get to that later, too) but some repairs to plumbing fixtures in the kitchens and bathrooms were required.

I had several contractors quote the cost of renovations and, all in all, the total cost to renovate was projected at about half of the purchase price. I had already spent five years fixing up my own home, with some pretty major renovations, so I felt confident that the renovation costs should not be a lot more than the price quotations, within reason.

The property was listed at an exceptionally low repossession price, so I decided to make an offer. I talked to the real estate agent and said I definitely wanted to purchase the property. It was suggested that since the price was so low, I should offer the bank the same amount that it was listed for. So that's what I did and that clinched the deal. One blight in the neighbourhood would be turned into a gem and I'd be rolling in dough, or so I thought!

Well, the contractor I selected was a relative of a friend, which normally would be the worst thing you could do. He had an excellent crew. Like all contractors, or at least in my experience, he was always complaining about something, mostly payments. We had agreed on a schedule of payments based on a timeline and the stages of work completion. He always wanted payment early, which I wouldn't do, so that led to some conflicts. I got through all the challenges and the project was only about 10% over budget. I was happy with the quality of work and pricing, but the contractor kept crying the blues about not making enough of a margin on the job. I figured – too bad, so sad - if he priced the job too low to not give himself enough profit then that was his problem.

I contracted the tear-down of the garage separately. The guy I hired said he would do it for a 24-pack of beer and figured it would only take him and his guys about six hours to complete. He was going to remove all the lumber and use it for some kind of project on his own property. Now this garage had to be at least sixty-years old. The roof was shot, and the wall boards didn't look too good to me but hey, he knows what he's doing, right! He turns up one morning in late November with a couple of guys who kind of looked like they might have lived there in one of the apartments at some point in the past. It was a cold, damp day with a light drizzle and these guys didn't look like they were in peak performance mode, at all.

After a couple of hours, the lead guy called and asked me to come over. When I got there, they had the roof off and had started on the walls. He said the job was a lot tougher than he thought it would be and that the wall boards didn't look like they were in very good shape. He asked me if I could give him the beer so they could have a couple and then finish the job. That really didn't sound like a successful plan, to say the least, so I told him I'd pay him when the job was finished. Those guys worked the whole day and got a big chunk of the work done. I could not believe they actually came back the next day to finish it off and collect their sack of beer.

I put the apartments up for rent and the bachelor was rented out right away. My first tenant! He was a recently divorced offshore oil rig worker making good wages doing the three week away/one week home shift. Good old "Tex" – *Perfect*, or so I thought! *He seemed like a nice guy, at the time.*

My general approach was going to be that my partner at the time would deal with the people issues of finding tenants, fielding complaints, collecting rent payments, evictions, etc. and I would handle the repair and maintenance issues. Let me tell you, *it doesn't work that way*! The tenants complain to the person they see around the property all the time mowing the lawn, fixing the fence or shovelling the driveway. What I'm saying is that I ended up getting it in both ears, and various other places too, if you know what I mean!

I ended up giving nicknames to many of the tenants, but not to their faces of course – I am Canadian after all. It was just my way of having a little snicker after having had an unpleasant exchange with one of them about some totally absurd complaint or bizarre situation I ended up in because of something stupid they did. And believe me, there were lots of them. Despite the problems they caused, I tried as much as I could to be respectful toward them. The times that I *was* direct with, or dismissive of, them would be when I reached the end of my very long fuse. We all have a breaking point, some shorter than others, but given that the three buildings I eventually owned were in somewhat rougher areas of town, I came to realize that these people had a lot more issues they were struggling with than paying the rent or being reasonable with their landlord.

# CHAPTER 2

# A Room with a View

The two-bedroom apartment in the front was beautifully remodeled and had a nice view of the park. It rented out right away to a nice couple in their mid-thirties with no kids. They got all their stuff moved in and I got a call from them after the wife had gotten in the shower. Apparently there was a serious water leak. I went over and saw that the water from the bathroom on the second floor, which was above the kitchen, came down through the kitchen ceiling when she turned on the shower. WTF!

After all that renovation, none of us thought to see if the *shower* worked properly. What happened was that the pipe from the tub faucet that ran up inside the wall to the showerhead was broken or detached. When the water-diverter on the tub faucet was pulled up, the water went into the broken pipe in the wall, and then had nowhere else to go except into the wall. Gravity being what it is… there you are with a seriously damaged kitchen ceiling, not to mention a tenant who is tired, sweaty and not the least bit impressed. The tickets I gave to them for the local sports facility to get cleaned up were appreciated and thankfully they were really good about it. *Aha*, a positive outcome in a bad situation. Maybe this tenant thing will be okay.

They didn't last too long though, because buddy got laid off and they couldn't pay the rent. They were good enough to tell me their situation and to move out, as opposed to stringing me along and trying to stay there and say they would make up the rents when they could. That never works out, as I was to find out many times in the future.

## "Sylvester"

During this same time the heavy spring rains were starting. The foundation was nearly one-hundred years old and made of stone, which was the same as all the houses around the park. It was built on a sloping rock ledge from back to front running down to the park. I had put a sump pump in the sump-hole in the basement floor, which was just rock ledge, not a poured concrete floor. I set the float level on the pump low enough so the pump would come on long before the water reached the bottom of the boiler or hot water heaters. The basement took on water, but the pump could handle the flow, as long as there was power. I decided to have some weeping-tile installed around the perimeter of the foundation, which did cut down on the water flow into the basement a bit. That was until more of the mortar between the stones started to deteriorate. During one storm I went over to check the basement, like I did on any heavy rains, and the pump wasn't working. The water had risen to a few inches *above* the bottom of the electric hot-water heaters. DAMN! I had another pump there, so I tried that out and it worked. The water cleared and all I had to do with the water heaters was change out the lower thermostat units in them.

I wondered why the pump had stopped working because it was fairly new, so I talked to a guy at the building supply center about it. He said that style of pump included a thermal shut-off feature so if the pump was working too much and began to overheat, it would shut off. *Aha*! Since I had two pumps and two hoses, I could put them both in the sump-hole, which was big enough, and set the float controls at different levels. That way if one pump went into thermal shut-off the other pump would kick in. *Perfect* – or so I thought!

Everything with the water problems was fine until a few years later. During one storm, as usual, I went to check the basement. The water was rising fast and neither pump was working. *Arrgh*! What now? - Don't panic. The water was getting close to the hot water heaters. I could get a bucket and start some hard labour carrying buckets up the narrow staircase, or I could try to figure out what the problem was. I decided to try the easy path. I saw that the breaker on the electrical panel had tripped off. Good, I reset the breaker and both pumps kicked in. Then the breaker tripped off again – maybe too much load on the circuit. I unplugged one of the pumps and reset the breaker again. That did the trick, the pump started again. The water level started to subside. The pump eventually went into thermal shut-off, so I unplugged it and plugged in the other pump. I got the water level down really low, but the water was coming into the basement way faster than I had ever seen before. I listened to hear where the water was coming in from and when I looked under a shelf along the wall, there was like a brook running through the foundation. Good Lord, some of the mortar must have let go and the water was flowing through the hole.

When the storm was over a couple of days later, I tried to figure out what to do. It looked like the hole was just below ground level on the outside, but I didn't know how in the world I was going to effectively plug it with mortar. I stewed on that for quite some time and then one night, after a few beers, I thought I had it! I figured I needed something that would easily spread out and fill any gaps in the hole. The next day I went out and got a can of instant-foam insulation. I went in the basement where I could clearly see where the hole was. I sprayed about half the can of foam in the hole and when it hardened up there was hardly a drop of water that came through the hole, even on the heaviest rainstorm.

Next, I had to set the sump pumps up so they ran off different circuits. That would work, as long as there was power. I had to install another outlet near the pumps, which took awhile. I usually kept the basement door closed when I was down there, but I was in and out so much that this time I must have forgotten and left it open. I finished the job, packed up my tools and materials, and went home. A couple of days later I was over there again and one of the neighbours asked if I had seen his cat. I told him I hadn't seen it and he said he thought it was in the basement. Of course I said – WHAT? He said he could hear a cat crying from in there.

We went over to where he thought it was and sure enough, we could hear it. I opened the basement door and let him go in and he came out with his cat, Sylvester, in his arms. Its claws were gone, and its paws were bloody. I knew there was a hole in the foundation above ground level on that side where we had heard the cat, and all I had done was jam some pink insulation in the hole to keep the cold air out. The cat must have found the hole and tried to claw its way out through it. It wouldn't have had any trouble getting something to drink because there was always a bit of water in the sump-hole, but I don't know how well it would have made out catching mice in the dark, with no claws.

The way the building was set up, none of the tenants had access to any parts of the basement. The water issues were in the part of the basement that was the original foundation directly below the two-bedroom unit. None of my problems in the basement affected or seemed to bother the tenants above, but they must have laughed to themselves to see me coming and going every time there was a heavy rain.

The foundation supporting the bachelor and one-bedroom apartments out back was poured concrete with a dirt floor, and the same width as the main house, about 22 feet wide. Many years back in the past there had been a one-storey kitchen extension added to the back of the original house, and it had caught fire some years ago. It had a foundation that was set in about four feet on either side from the line of the house foundation, and it wasn't removed when the new foundation was poured. That meant that there was about a 2-foot wide crawl space between the two foundations. There were holes punched through each side of the old foundation wall in order to access the dirt floor under the bachelor apartment. There were no pipes or wiring under there, so I didn't know why that was done, and seriously wish it hadn't been!

One of the tenants in the bachelor apartment was complaining that the floor was cold. Still not knowing where to draw the line with tenants, I decided to investigate. I shinnied along the crawl space, which I could barely fit through, with a flashlight. I could see that there was no insulation under the floor. With an amount of contortionism I didn't know I was capable of, I could get through the hole in the foundation wall. I was able to push bags of pink insulation through the crawl space and into the space below the apartment. There was about 4-feet of headroom in there so all the work installing the insulation had to be done while I was laying on my back.

There wasn't any natural light in there, so I had to drag a trouble light in with me. I was more worried about the critters that might be in there than what my real concern should have been. It met the criteria for a confined space. It was big enough to have enough oxygen and was open on either side through the crawl spaces, but I shouldn't have been working in there without a ventilator. I got one from work, made sure I had some airflow, and got the job done after three or four long nights, but it didn't matter. The tenant said it was still too cold and moved out. *Arrgh*! I never heard another complaint from any other tenant about the floor being cold, though.

## "Marge & Homer"

Another couple moved into the 2-bedroom unit right away, a similar situation as the first tenants, but younger and with no kids. They had one of those funny relationships. The verbal jabs at each other were constant, but it all appeared to be in good humour, and taken that way, I think. It almost seemed like a little friendly competition to see who could come up with the wittiest line. It wasn't like couples you're around who bicker at each other all the time and you feel uncomfortable around them. Marge or Homer would just say it and it was history. I wondered sometimes if they really even heard each other, because some of the things they said to each other were very bizarre, but funny too.

They were both wonderful, reasonable people. "Homer" was in the insurance industry and his wife "Marge" was doing child-care for a few kids. She ended up looking after mine fairly often. She used to take all the kids out in the back yard and let them play in a little splash-pool. One day she asked if I could build a higher fence out back. The neighbour's fence that was there seemed okay, so I asked her what the problem was. She said there were a couple of pit-bull terriers in the other yard across the back fence and she was worried that they could jump over it. She told me that the dogs fought quite a bit and that the owner even encouraged them to fight.

I understood what her concern was, because I don't trust those dogs either (and I trust their owners even less!).

The property alignment out back was such that there were two properties abutting my back fence, both rental houses. They were separated from each other by a fence which attached, more or less in the middle, to my fence.

Homer helped me put up a higher fence, on the left-side where the dogs were, on my side of the property line. It turned out a few months later that the dogs escaped out through the front of their property, ran about eight blocks away and attacked a woman in her yard. The police came and shot one of the dogs and managed to take the other one away. We heard that the owner of the dogs already had an order against him for not being allowed to own dogs. After he got his sweet little slap on the wrist from the courts, he went right out and got two more dogs. It seems he must have had *something* in his house worth protecting, so I just left it at putting up the fence – that was the only action I was going to take!

One summer I ended up golfing with Homer quite a bit. The great thing about that was that he was way worse than me. I would be struggling to shoot a legitimate 100 (remember I'm a rule follower) and he would be struggling to cheat his score to 120. We got along fine until he started to cause the tenant out back, "Tex", some trouble. There was some petty drama going on between them for some reason and Homer tried to draw me into it. He seemed to think that since we golfed together, I would side with him and give Tex the boot, which is what he wanted. I didn't bite and told him to work out their problems between them. After that we still got along alright, but never went golfing together. I never liked playing with cheaters anyway.

Marge and Homer were there for about five years and were good tenants who never really caused any problems, and were incredibly good to my children. Unfortunately for them, or so it seemed at the time, I had to give them notice to move since I was going to move in after my divorce. It turned out that they said it was the best thing that could've happened to them. They found a beautiful home in a nice neighbourhood and bought it. I saw them a few times later over the years and they seemed very happy, but probably were still sparring with each other on a regular basis. Which, of course, kept them happy.

## "Captain Crunch"

A few years later I had a problem with the back fence on the right-hand side of the property. The guy renting that property had been there for years with his wife and were very friendly. I'm not sure what kind of business he was in, and frankly I didn't want to know. He had three sons who were full grown, very full grown! One of my neighbours told me that one was in prison for murder, one was in for manslaughter, and the other one, who was living with them, just got out for drug trafficking. Oh-oh!

I used to shovel the driveway, which was one-hundred feet long with parking for three cars. What a job that was! The driveway was so narrow that I couldn't find a guy with a plow who was game to do it. But at least I figured out what I was in for whenever it snowed. It seemed to take about one hour of shovelling for every five centimeters of snow. So, on a twenty centimeter snowfall, there goes four hours of my time. Anything over that, well, time to do it in shifts.

I eventually found a guy who would plow it and he was plowing the snow all the way back to the fence. This particular year we had tons of snow. The fence was only womanized 4x8 lattice panels, and of course they gave way. The next fall I decided to fix the fence. It didn't matter to me that much because that area was kind of hidden by lots of small trees and vegetation, but I wanted to keep their dog out of my yard. A couple of weeks after I finished rebuilding it, I was out back doing some yard work. There was a very big angry guy across the fence who seemed to be talking to himself, I hoped! He was one of the sons of the neighbour out back. That continued for awhile and I finished what I was doing. I went and grabbed a beer and noticed he was still ranting and raving. By now it was clear that it was something to do with the fence.

God help me why I do this stuff, but I thought I should go over and see what was bothering him. I went over and said, "Hi neighbour". DOH! He went off on me about not asking him about repairing the fence before I did it. I apologized and said I thought they would think it would look better. He must have spent some time at sea, because he used some expressions that even *I* never heard before. I apologized again, but said I thought it would be better for our security to keep our dogs in our yards. He actually told me that it was worse, because now *he had no way to get out of his back yard.* WHAT! Oh right, silly me - I had blocked his escape route. Fearing he'd get out his rusty razor, I set sail for calmer waters.

## "The Birdman of Buctouche"

After several years of living in the two-bedroom unit, I decided to start looking for another house of my own. Enough equity had built up that I thought it was time to add some more debt and make a move. I really loved living on the park, but having tenants living in the same building was kind of getting on my nerves. I found a nice one and a half storey house not too far away and in a nice area that I liked. It was vacant but had a basement apartment that was rented out to a woman and her young son.

There had been some significant improvements to the property, which included a metal roof, a serious HVAC system, and a huge garage with an upper loft. The house had hardwood floors on the main and upper levels that needed refinishing and new-style hardwood flooring in the lower apartment. It also needed a complete interior paint job. Other than that, it was in good condition. It also had cedar shingles on the exterior, which I liked, and there was a little wishing well on the front lawn. It had been on the market for awhile, so I put in an offer and secured the purchase.

I advertised the two-bedroom unit at Johnny's for rent, and got the renovations going at the new house. I slowly began moving things over there, since I was not in a big hurry. I still had some odds-and-ends scattered mostly on the living room and dining room floors when I got a call Sunday morning from a guy that wanted to see the apartment. I hadn't really cleaned the place up yet, but I said I'd meet him there.

He and his wife showed up in their over-sized pick-up truck with a great big trailer attached to the back. That looked kind of funny to me. Turned out it *was* kind of funny. I showed them around the apartment and yard, and they said they wanted it – *right away*. Meaning that very moment! I wasn't really ready for that, so I asked him what his situation was. He said both he and his wife, who could not hear nor speak very well, worked at the same company in northern New Brunswick and had both been transferred to the company's head office in Dartmouth. They were staying in a motel for the time being and wanted to unload all their stuff in the trailer immediately. It was the strangest situation, but how could it not be true, two people travelling around with all their worldly possessions hooked to the back of their truck. I took it on gut instinct that they were both working and could afford the place. They certainly *seemed like a nice couple, at the time*.

I decided to let them take it, so I bagged up the rest of the stuff I had there and apologized profusely that the apartment wasn't as clean as I would like. They didn't care about that at all. I called their employer the next day and confirmed their employment and salaries. We did up the lease that night and they were good to go. They were a nice couple but had some "interesting" touches to the décor of the apartment. It was kind of off-beat, even a little strange, all revolving around Harley Davidsons, one of which he owned, and eagles. It seemed to work for them though, and I kinda thought it reflected who they were.

All in all, they were a fine couple and good tenants. He had some odd quirks about him but given what I'd been through with some of the other tenants, they were great, until Spring arrived. There was a huge tree out back, the tallest one in the neighbourhood, about eighty-feet tall. Birdman always parked his precious truck out back because he didn't want it out front where someone might steal it. That made it hard for the other tenants to park, because the truck was just so big, but they all seemed to work around that somehow. One day I was over mowing the lawn and he came up to me and started complaining about all the birds crapping on his truck. I just commented that there seemed to be more birds than any other year, and I left it at that. There didn't seem to be that much crap on his truck anyway, maybe a half-dozen spots.

The next time I was over he was like a wild man. His truck was totally splattered with bird droppings, and I mean there was A LOT. I almost burst out laughing, it was *so* bad, but then thought better of it, given his state of mind. He told me that I'd have to get up in the tree and hang some shiny things, like CDs, from the branches to scare the birds away. He said if I didn't, he was going to make me pay for the cost of washing his truck. I told him my pole-climbing days were well behind me, and my tree climbing days were even further back than that! I was just waiting for his next line – hire a falcon! But it never came because, luckily for me, and unluckily for him, within about a month the company they worked at went out of business and they both were laid off. They moved out and headed back to New Brunswick. *Au revoir, mes amies!*

## "The Druid"

I really didn't know what the call her: "Mustang Sally"? "The Vet"? "Olive Oil"? I do know one thing though - she couldn't stop talking! I'd never heard anyone talk that much, enough to make your head spin. You ever listen to an album played backwards? Now and again you think you might have heard something intelligible, and usually scary, but you weren't quite sure what it was - it was like that.

The Druid and her two "boyfriends" arrived at the apartment to meet me for a viewing. She was tall and as skinny as a beanpole, her current boyfriend looked like he'd just gotten off the set of "Alaska Bush People", and her former boyfriend looked like he was from the cast of "Glee". Each to his own – I say. They were all working, and *seemed like a nice triad, at the time.*

She asked if it was okay to have a dog and I asked her how big it was. My main concern with dogs was if I'd be attacked by one if I came over to the property. She said she had two pugs. Ha ha - no problem there. She told me she also had a cat and a couple of gerbils. She talked so much and so fast that I must have missed something during the conversation, but I think I heard something about "I love animals".

They moved in and, as usual, she called me over to fix a couple of minor things. OMG! It was like a menagerie in there. She could have been open for business as a pet store. There were birds, fish, rodents, reptiles, felines, canines. "Wild Kingdom" had nothing on her. I could only imagine the scene if any of those cages got open, something right out of "Dexter"! There were bags of pet food and straw everywhere. I suppose it satisfied Bushman, at least it gave him something to stick between his teeth.

It was none of my concern, right. The dogs were not big enough to get their mouths around my big toe, and she assured me that the snakes were not the poisonous type. Oh, Happy Day!

Their choice of décor was unusual, if not spooky. There was a montage of Stonehenge sketches and paintings of odd-looking characters who were either soothsayers, sorcerers, or David Bowie - I couldn't quite tell. Her art reflected the way she talked, I was never quite sure what was going on in her head, or on her walls! Some of it was downright pornographic, I think, in an artistic kind of way, of course.

Glee-boy moved out within two months and Bushman shortly after. This looked like trouble. A single Druid at a part-time job with sixteen mouths to feed. Oh right, no wonder she was so skinny!

She couldn't afford the rent, and she couldn't possibly get any skinnier, so she gave me notice to move out. I never, in my wildest dreams, thought I might need a lawn mower to clean up a livingroom, but I considered it. I told her I wasn't going to give her the damage deposit back. She was only there for about five months, so she wanted to "talk it over". There wasn't any rational reason for me giving it back, but I think there were references to her father being a lawyer…she didn't damage the place… she didn't cause any trouble. It's not that my memory isn't clear, it's just that she talked so friggin' much that I had no clear idea at the time what she was saying. "Mustang Sally, think you better slow your Mustang down"! Speaking of which…

She had the two pugs with her as we were standing out front talking this over. A car came flying down the street at the time, imagine that - a Mustang! I love those cars. One of the dogs ran onto the street. OMG! – flattened like a pancake! JEEEZUZ! Is that something you'd call ironic? I'm not sure, but you could definitely call it horrific, horrendous, devastating, sad…take your pick.

What could I do? Well, you know the old saying (very old, in fact) – "You can't kick a Druid when they're down!" I told her I'd give the deposit back. I suppose it wasn't enough to cover the Druid burial ceremony to follow, but she'd probably have to wait for the summer solstice for that! Give her some time to save up some *dinero*.

# CHAPTER 3

# The Treehouse

**"Tex" – Part 1**

When he moved in to the one-bedroom unit there were no problems, for awhile. The apartment was very secluded at the back of the building, with big trees surrounding the back yard. One evening I was at the building a little late doing something or other and he came staggering up the driveway. Well, no problem there. He was on his days off and had been out having a few too many beers after three weeks of hard work on the rig. After a few months of seeing similar behaviour, I came to realize that he was binge drinking in order to make up for the three weeks of abstinence on the rig. That was still not any concern of mine. He wasn't bothering any of the other tenants or causing any disturbance to the neighbours, so that was his business.

Over the first three or four years he became friends with a few of the neighbours, who were married and owned their own homes. The guys he met liked to get out of the house and enjoy their beer. I could tell because I'd be over at the building different times doing yard work or some repairs, and they'd be up on the big back deck of Tex's apartment having a great time. I was friends with one of the guys, and one time he invited me up for a beer, but I really didn't think that was such a good idea. Tex was friendly enough, always paid his rent, and never caused any trouble, but I'd noticed his behaviour was changing. He seemed to be talking much louder than usual and was more argumentative. When he did laugh, it was explosive. He also seemed to be around a lot more.

### *"The Front Row Seat"*

Around this time, several years after Tex moved in, I got divorced (as I mentioned earlier) and moved into the two-bedroom unit out front, so now I could witness the show first-hand, on a full-time basis!

It turned out that Tex had been laid-off work due to a down-turn in the industry. He still paid his rent on time, but his car wasn't working. Apparently, he always took his daughter out on Sundays at two o'clock for her horseback riding lessons, and one day he asked me if he could borrow my car until he got his repaired. He was sober and we were on good terms, so I felt bad for him and, because – *he seemed like a nice guy*! - I gave him my spare key and off he went. They came back later that day and his daughter thanked me so much for doing that.

The next Sunday I went to get in the car at about 2:30 and it was gone! At first, I thought it was stolen, but it was there in the morning when I looked out, and it wasn't much of a car. It was old and not in very good condition, so I couldn't imagine anyone wanting to steal it, especially in broad daylight. Then I thought again. I didn't get my spare key back from Tex the last Sunday, so I started to wonder if he took the car. I decided to wait it out for a bit and see what would happen and, sure enough, he drives up at around 4:30, all smiles that he got his daughter to her riding lesson. Good Lord, what do you do with that! I couldn't say much in front of his daughter. But I sure had something to say after she left, though. I asked him what in the world he was thinking about by just taking off in my car. He said he had asked me if he could use it to take his daughter to her lessons *until he got his car fixed*, and since his car still wasn't fixed, and since I had left him the key.......JEEEZUZ! Perfectly rational behaviour as far as he was concerned.

Okay, time to create some distance here. No more car for you, buddy!

**"Shrek"**

One of Tex's neighbour friends across the park, "Shrek", had built a garage that in fact was really a man-cave. Both of them had invited me to come over different nights to "have a couple of beers". I knew what that meant, and it didn't sound like a good idea to me, so I never went over.

A year or so later one of tenants in the bachelor apartment was a younger guy who played the guitar a lot. He was working full-time and *he seemed like a nice guy*. Which in this case he actually was. I had worked hard in the yard all day one Saturday when he was home, and when I finished up, he offered me a beer and suggested we go over to Shrek's garage after supper. He said they were going to get out the guitars and have a little jam session. I knew he was a normal guy so I figured he probably wouldn't stay really late and I could leave when he did. I had some bongo drums, so I decided to give it a go. I wanted to see what the place was like anyway, but mostly I wanted to see what kind of characters were hanging out there. I was sure it would be an experience to remember!

The "cave" had a high-end music system, a pool table, and of course a fridge. It even had an upper level with a couple of couches, a pinball machine, and another fridge. I don't know what the couches were used for, maybe sleeping, but thought it better not to sit on them. It was clear that no vehicles were going to be spending any time in that building.

So, I knew going in that there would be some real interesting characters there. I was fool enough not to think that through. I walked in and there was Tex, *Oh-oh*! Then I saw one of my former tenants that I had evicted about a year before. *Double oh-oh*! As a tenant, he had been drinking and raising hell out back in the bachelor apartment for about nine months. I had begun to worry about my two young daughters being exposed to that, so I gave him notice to move out. He left on bad terms, of course. He was kind of a big guy, so I said hello and he kind of grunted. I think he said, "Hi *Ethel*" – well, you know what I thought. Whatever he said, I was just glad he never put the boots to me, and thankfully the guys got the music going right away.

Nobody could really play anything other than the guitar player, who was pretty good. He played quite a few tunes, and everyone was merrily drinking away, singing along at times. After quite awhile, Shrek must have got his courage up. He said he could play the guitar, so he grabbed it, instead of just asking for it, and started out on his "performance". You know how sometimes somebody is doing something so pitiful that you actually feel embarrassed *yourself.* Well this was one of those moments. Shrek was in his glory playing the first 4 or 8 bars of every song he ever started to learn, but never finished learning. He never sang a note but kept looking up at us every now and again with his one wandering eye to see how impressed we were. I thought I did well to sneak away before midnight and, needless to say, I never went back. Apparently, these guys did this a lot, because many nights, while sitting out in my sunporch, I would see Tex traipsing across the park going to Shrek's for another bout of heavy drinking.

## "Tex" – Part 2

A year or so after that, Tex began (or was already in the middle of) a long, slow descent into self-destruction. I'd be doing yard work, or hanging the laundry on the line out back, or something else, and I'd hear these loud heated conversations he would be having on the phone. I pieced together that the arguments were with his ex-wife about money. These calls became more frequent and more vocal. His ex-wife, who I had met when he first moved in and they were still on good terms, actually called me one day. She said that he had run out of unemployment benefits a long time ago and was not paying child support for their teenage daughter. She told me that he had used up his daughter's education fund, which she said was a substantial amount of money – in the 10s of thousands of dollars. I don't know what she wanted from me, other than a shoulder to cry on (figuratively) but there was nothing I could do to make the situation better. Maybe she thought Tex and I were close friends or something, and that I could talk to him about things, which wasn't going to happen – *at all*!

The arguments and shouting on the phone got really bad after that, and then all of a sudden it stopped. He asked me one day if he could use my cell phone to make a call, so I asked him why he couldn't call from his apartment. He said his phone had been cut off, *Aha*! This could be trouble. No unemployment cheque, no funds to draw on. Hmm?

Soon after, sure enough, he missed his rent payment. He said he was looking for work but being in his midfifties I knew it was going to be tough. We were still on good terms, so I let it slide for the month. He had been living there for more than six years and had never missed a rent payment. He never caused any trouble with the neighbours either, so I figured that was fair enough. He missed the next month's rent too but had found a warehouse job through contacts in the oilfield industry. He only got enough pay to keep his head above water, for awhile. I don't know how he kept his drinking under control enough to get to work every day, but he did it for about ten months. I guess it was just long enough to put in another claim for his unemployment cheques, which he promptly did after he got laid-off again. In the meantime, he couldn't pay off the back-rent, so I cut a deal with him. My apartment needed a paint job, so he painted the whole place out "for free". He wasn't a master painter for sure, but it did look better when he finished.

I knew the situation with Tex was going to go bad, meaning not paying the rent, as soon as his unemployment ran out again. He was binge drinking until his unemployment money for the month ran out, and his behavior was becoming bizarre. He never bothered me and mostly kept to himself (and Shrek's) but I was worried he might drop a cigarette or something and burn the place down. I had to do something to get him moved out, so I decided to raise his rent. I wrote in the rental increase notice (prescribed by the regulations, of course!) that since the rent had not increased in eight years, it was going up by $100 per month. He went ballistic. Yelling. Crying, Whimpering. "OH, woe is me!" and "You scoundrel, you prick!" (well, it was much more colourful language than that!).

He eventually settled down and wanted me to come up to his apartment and talk things over. I didn't think that was such a good idea, not that I was afraid of him physically, but I did want to see the condition of the apartment. I went up and the place was an absolute pigsty. Here was someone who did nothing all day, every day, and couldn't lift a finger to clean the dishes, floors, or any other surface I saw. God only knew what the bathroom was like. I sat on the couch, with some trepidation, and we talked a bit. I felt something on my ankles and when I looked down, there were literally hundreds of fleas jumping up out of the carpet. I had to get out of there, and so did he!

My fuse ran out not long after that. I was going out to my car one Saturday morning and Tex came down the driveway. He looked really agitated. I thought - what now? He said he was in a hurry and needed a lift. I asked him where he needed to go, and he said he had to go to the Jerry Springer Show. Of course, I said, "What are you talking about?" as he was trying to open the back door of my car. He said that he was going to be a guest on the show, and he was late, so I needed to get him there right away. WHOA Tex! You're losing your marbles, which is exactly what I told him. He must have been hallucinating because he walked back up the driveway and then tried to climb over the back fence, maybe to try and solicit a ride from the neighbour there.

I thought he needed medical attention, so I called 911. I explained the situation and they asked me a lot about his behavioural history, age, height, weight, etc. They said they would send a team over. Oh, they sent a team alright! The police showed up and talked the situation over with me. They went out back and they found him in his apartment. When the police returned to the front of the house, they told me that he seemed stable. They explained the reason that they were there was that emergency health services can't enter a situation like that without the police doing an assessment. Oh great, now he thinks I called the cops on him, which is exactly what he said to me when I saw him the next day.

I found out from one of the Shrek boys a few days later that Tex had talked to him about what had happened. I knew this guy for a long time and knew Tex trusted him. It turned out that he advised Tex to move out, which thankfully he did the next month. I say thankfully, until I was faced with cleaning and repairing the apartment! *Adios amigo!*

## "The Dealer"

Another tenant who took over the apartment after my "Pacific Heights" tenant (who I'll get to later) was a woman who was about 30 years old and was working two part-time jobs. She was just on minimum wage, but her references were good, and they both said she always picked up extra shifts, plus she got her tips. She looked pretty tough, but that was just on the outside, right. *She seemed like a nice person, at the time. Perfect -* or so I thought!

I was still living in the two-bedroom unit out front at this point. It was probably a year after she moved in that I noticed some odd behaviour happening. A lot of different rough looking guys started coming up the driveway, separately, for 5 or 10-minute visits. This was happening on a regular basis, and I was kind of worried about how long it would be before the police showed up.

She came down to see me one night and told me that her entrance door "wasn't working". Yeah, right. It looked like somebody had taken a crowbar to it and tried to pry it open, but they weren't successful. When I called the police, you should have seen the look on her face, absolute horror. She never said a word to me and when the cops arrived, she never said a word to them either. One of the cops looked it over and said that was one hell of a good deadbolt because normally they should have gotten through it.

I was able to fix it up enough that the door worked okay, but it still looked damaged. She asked me if I was going to get a new door, and I told her I would - when she stopped dealing drugs.

Nothing changed as far as her visitors were concerned, so I gave her notice to vacate shortly after that. It sure was uncomfortable, to put it mildly, that last month anytime our paths crossed, and anytime I saw those guys around.

## CHAPTER 4

# The Revolving Door

**"The Gamblers"**

Kenny, his girlfriend, and their dog were some of the first tenants in the bachelor apartment. I never thought about not allowing dogs but didn't think they'd last very long in that small apartment anyway. They were just a work-a-day couple with regular jobs who had enough for their lifestyle. The dog was a big German Shephard. It was friendly enough, but you'd never know it. It had a loud bark and barked a lot when anyone came around. Even when it knew me well it would bark at me, and when I was working around the place it would continue to bark.

Kenny would tie it to a long rope through the day. The rope was long enough to almost get to the bottom of the driveway, maybe about eight feet back from the sidewalk. The houses were so close together that if anyone was walking along the sidewalk, they wouldn't be able to see the dog. I can't count the number of times I saw people nearly have a heart attack when they got near the driveway. The dog always picked the exact worst moment to lay into it. It would start barking and absolutely scare the bejeezus out of anyone who walked by.

They stayed there for five years in that little apartment, always paid their rent, and spent all their free time gambling at the VLTs. They never really drank much or caused any problems, but eventually moved in with a friend who had bought a house.

After The Gamblers moved out, the bachelor apartment was like a revolving door with tenants, and I could understand why. It had a good layout and was a nice situation facing the back yard. But it didn't get much sun because of all the trees, and it was pretty small. There was really no room for storage either. I came to accept the fact that the tenants were good for about 12-18 months (but that didn't necessarily mean 12-18 months of rent payments). They were just looking for something to get started with their first apartment that was cheap, or more likely, as it turned out, they were looking to escape from some situation they had been in.

### "Babe Ruth"

One of the tenants who rented the bachelor apartment was a small younger guy, maybe twenty-two years old or so. He got back on his rent fairly soon into the lease. I got some calls from the other tenants complaining about a lot of shouting from the apartment. They thought another guy was living there with Babe, which wasn't permitted in the lease. They didn't think it was arguing but said it could possibly have been some sort of sexual acrobatics. I didn't want to get involved *in that*, so I just told them to call the police if there was a disturbance coming from the apartment.

Babe eventually got more behind on the rent and I had some heated exchanges with him. One night I asked a friend to come over because I had given Babe an eviction notice and he hadn't moved out. We went to the back door and knocked on it several times. He finally shouted through the door, telling me to F-off. I told him we needed to talk, but he wouldn't have any of it, so I told him I had a key and was going to come in. He warned me that if I came in the apartment, he had a Louisville Slugger waiting there with my name on it. My buddy looked at me and suggested we get out of there, *pronto*, which we did!

I looked at the Regulations to see what I could do. I had to file a claim for non-payment of rent and a hearing would be scheduled with the Tenancy Board. I did that and the hearing was scheduled for *three weeks later*. Babe was already one month in arrears so that didn't sound too promising. I had to serve him notice of the hearing and I was able to corner him one day in the driveway and give it to him.

I went to the hearing and he didn't show up. I presented my case and the adjudicator said he would mail his decision to me and Babe *within two weeks*. WHAT? I told the adjudicator that I was already out a month's rent, and that would take it into the next month. My question, of course, was - "What will I do if he still doesn't move out"? He said the Regulations provide for the Sheriff to remove the tenant if that happened. All I would need to do was pay the application fee and they would schedule the eviction, which would probably be within one month of receiving the application. OH HO! So that's a nice, tidy process. If a tenant wants to put it to you, it really takes about three months to get them out. Sweet! So much for the landlord having all the power. I'll end up becoming *very* familiar with this process in the future.

Over the years, I ended up talking to a woman who was a lawyer who also had some rental units. She said she just hires two great big guys and sends them around to *motivate* the offending tenant to move, immediately, and that they would be changing the locks the next evening. Worked every time, she said. I don't think that is what you would call your "due process", more like what you would call your "process due"! Sounded like a viable plan, but not for me. Remember, I'm a rule follower – or maybe to put it another way, a sucker.

## "Maurice Chevalier"

Maurice was a cool cat, smooth as silk alright. He had the gift of the gab with a slight French accent. He would break out into song every once in awhile and he didn't sound to bad, actually. He had a great job with a great salary, confirmed by his employer. He was the top salesman for a national medical supply company. For some reason he showed me a bunch of promotion materials and samples he had in his trunk, syringes, vials, packs of powders and crystalline looking substances. He had the image of a sales guy, too, and didn't look like a pusher, but I had to wonder. He had the stylish pointy-toed shoes, pressed trousers, casual but business-like sports jacket, and white button-down shirt opened at the top. This guy looked like a dream tenant. And... *he seemed like a nice guy, at the time.*

So, Maurice moves in. *Perfect* - or so I thought!

When a tenant moves out, the power company offered an arrangement called the Landlord Meter Plan. That allows the landlord to keep the power on in the apartment until a new tenant moves in. The billing goes to the landlord until the new tenant switches it over to their name. Usually I liked to have that done within a few days of move-in.

Maurice was there for a week and I called the power company to see if the account had been changed, and they said it had not. I called Maurice and he said he hadn't gotten to that yet but would do it right away. It was getting on to mid-June at this point. I checked with the power company a couple of days later and he still hadn't changed the account to his name. In fact, the agent said there was an embargo on him. Wait a minute - what the hell does that mean? The agent said he was in arrears on another account and they wouldn't supply power to him.

Okay, I needed to think about this. Here's a guy who in every way appears to be successful. Hold on, what's he doing renting out a little four-hundred square foot bachelor apartment hidden away in Dartmouth...and he can't get power? He should be renting a penthouse suite somewhere in downtown Halifax.

I went to talk to him the next night. He came clean about it and said that he'd had a restaurant business with a partner, and when they closed it, they owed $1000 to the power company that they didn't pay. He said he was working to pay it off and would get the power in the apartment switched into his name when that was done. *In the meantime*, he asked if I could keep the power in my name, and he'd pay me when the bill came.

You know how you meet swindlers, and you know they're swindlers. You can tell they're trying to pull a fast one and they just can't hide it. A con man is different - very unassuming and not the least bit brash or boastful. They don't start out pushing things too far. They just need the first hook, then they'll add the line and sinker! That was Maurice through and through.

Since…*he seemed like a nice guy*, I agreed to keep the power in my name and get him to pay the bill until he got things sorted out.

Now we were coming in to heating season. He had left (or lost) his job and was starting a new one, so he was behind on paying what he owed me for the power bill. This could get expensive. He had one excuse after another: I'm trying to pay off the power company, I need to get my car fixed, Yadda, Yadda, Yadda. Here we go. It was mid-November and OOPS! - my fuse ran out.

I told him that I was going to have the power disconnected. It's absolutely amazing how these people can come up with stories in an instant. He said he was getting ready to go to Calgary to live with his former fiancée. They were going to get married! He said he would appreciate it *if I'd leave the power on* until he left at the end of the month. Good Lord! He never even thought about at least throwing me a bone, like – I'll pay you back when I get working in Calgary. I suppose other things would get in the way of that, like the wedding costs, the plane ticket, the honeymoon, Yadda, Yadda, Yadda.

I knew there were regulations around the power company terminating service during the cold weather season. But the power was in my name, and the lease with Maurice said he was responsible for the service. I called the power company and talked it over with them. I was told that I could connect or disconnect the service whenever I wanted, so I put a disconnect order in for the apartment. It was scheduled for the following Friday, three days out. *Perfect* - or so I thought!

I went over to the building late in the day on Friday and the power was still connected. I called the power company and they said they had disconnected the power earlier in the day. The technician said a guy approached him and said he was living there, so he reconnected the power. I told the agent on the phone that my order stood and that I wanted that power shut off by the end of the day! The agent assured me that that would happen, and it did. I was there when the technician came, and so was Maurice. He was pretty agitated but didn't say anything.

I went over to the building on Sunday and he told me he was freezing his *cajones* off. He actually had the gall to say that it was pretty low of me to disconnect the power. I just rubbed my chin and said, *"au revoir,* Ethel!" He was out two days later. *Hasta la vista, baby!*

## "Squirt"

After Maurice moved out I got a call from Social Services about an ad for the bachelor apartment. He had a client who had moved to the city from Winnipeg. He was staying at the Salvation Army at the time and they were looking to get him set up in an apartment.

They came over for a viewing. They liked the place and his worker said that Social Services would pay the rent by direct deposit. He signed a one-year lease and, since the apartment was vacant, he moved in right away. He didn't have much stuff, but his worker was going to help him out with furnishing the place.

He was a sweet little man, barely 5' nothin, who was retired and on a small pension. He had a daughter living in the area, so he moved to Dartmouth to be near her. He was almost like a character out of Seinfeld: a low-talker, very demure. Whenever I was talking to him, I was always waiting for his head to retract into his body, like a turtle.

After about five months his worker called and said that even though Squirt liked the apartment, he found himself isolated from the friends he had made in Halifax. His worker was giving notice, on Squirt's behalf, to vacate the apartment. I asked him if Social Services would cover the rent for the remainder of the lease, but he said *he didn't have the authority* to do that. I just love the way those guys talk!

## "Igor"

The bachelor apartment was up for rent again after Squirt moved out. Finances were a bit tight at the time and I made a bad decision that I knew I'd regret. A cab driver came over to view it. He took the application and said he'd bring it back. When he came back, there was a pretty substantial looking Russian guy (Igor) with him, at least that's what his accent sounded like. He had to be 6'3" and about 240lbs. The cabbie had the application filled out and gave it to me. The Russian didn't say much but said he'd be covering the rent. I asked if I should put his name on the lease too – *Ho-Ho-Ho*, how silly of me! Igor gave me a sneer as he peeled off the deposit and first month's rent from a wad of bills he pulled out of his pocket.

I could tell right there that there would be no credit checks, no reference checks, and no discussion whatever about the situation at all. I also knew that this was going to go south, probably real fast. That's the only thing I was right about that day.

I assumed that Igor must have been giving the hack money for the rent because, thankfully, I never saw him again. He was one scary looking dude. The cabbie was giving me money orders for the rent every month for eight months or so. Then it happened, as I knew it would. He didn't have the rent for the next month. Igor must have cut him loose.

After a tenant is fifteen days in arrears you could give them an eviction notice, which I did. I couldn't believe that he moved out at the end of the month and didn't cause me any grief by going through "the process". He left all his stuff in the apartment. I soon found out why he seemed so distant and unresponsive whenever I talked to him. I found a journal he was keeping, and it really looked like he was suffering from severe depression and was on the verge of doing himself in.

I didn't know what to do with his stuff, not that there was a lot of it. Now I found out that there was another twist to the Regulations when I looked up what to do. It said you have to catalog and store all of their possessions for six months after they move out. Then you need to make documented attempts to return it to them. Well, there hadn't been many tenants who gave me a forwarding address, so I looked through everything that was there trying to find some useful information. I didn't find a forwarding address, but I did find the money order for the last month's rent, *Yahoo*! I promptly went to the bank and cashed it. All I could figure is that he must have misplaced it amongst all the junk in his apartment and was so mixed up in his personal fog that he couldn't get out of his own way. I felt bad for him but all I could do was put all his stuff in the shed. He never came back for it, so six months later I set it all out in the trash.

## "The Girlfriend"

A woman in her mid-forties moved in next. She wasn't there a week before she started in on me. The first issue was that there were ants in the closet. I went over to look at the situation and didn't see any, but I put down an ant trap in the closet and one outside each entrance door. She called a few days later and said the ants were still there. When I went over she showed me that there was a gap with an opening to the basement under the carpet in the closet. I got some spray-on insulation and filled the hole, but I still didn't see any ants.

The next thing was a couple of light bulbs blew. Since she just moved in, I figured I was responsible for that, or at least didn't mind changing them out. When I got there, she was concerned that there was an electrical fault. Oh, come on now, it was just a couple of bulbs that went out, okay!

The third thing was that the weatherstripping around the side entrance door didn't look too good to her. She was worried that when the weather turned cold there would be a draft coming in. Yeah, I thought – if you last until then!

The fourth thing was the side deck. It was barely 12" high with two steps and about 10' wide. One of the treads on the bottom step was split a little bit on one end, but the whole tread was solidly nailed on and not a hazard at all, from my point of view. Given that the stairs were so wide it was pretty easy to avoid that little part that was split. I changed it out anyway.

The fifth thing was……

The sixth thing was…..

The seventh thing was……

This went on over the summer and was constant. I was over there once or twice a week "responding to her needs".

One day I was over there, and she said "Kevin, we need to talk". *Dios mio!* What do you want now, woman?

She was sitting on her back deck and she actually said to me "come over here and sit down", as she patted the empty chair next to her. WTF? Okay, I've been here before, and it ain't a good place to be!

She said, "I don't think our relationship is working out". Double WTF! You know about that fuse I talked about? Well, that was it. I said, "listen to this *Girlfriend*, give me notice to move out right away because I'm not putting up with any of your wacko s**t anymore". She was astounded that I could be so "hurtful", but she did move out at the end of the next month. Breaking up is hard to do!

### "The Happy Hippies"

Hippy-chick was in her mid-fifties and lived about an hour-and-a-half drive from the city. She wanted a little place to stay through the week while she was working in town. She planned on going home for the weekends and maybe the odd night through the week. She had a good job at a big company with a good salary. *Perfect* - or so I thought!

I met her husband when he helped her move in. *They seemed like a nice couple, at the time.*

We did an inspection of the apartment and the only existing damage was some small tearing in the carpet near the back door. It was about six-inches in diameter where the "Girlfriend's" cat was scratching at it to try and get out the door. That was no problem and noted on the inspection report. She had a few complaints when she first moved in but that was normal, just a couple of things she wanted done.

Her husband came to town now and again and they used to sit out on the back deck a lot, smoking some of that funny stuff. She asked me if I could put an awning or something over top of their deck so they could sit out when it was raining. She'd been a good tenant and was always paying the rent on time so I figured I'd see what I could do. The cost wasn't too bad, but putting it up was quite a struggle, given that I was working alone doing an overhead job. It worked out okay after a long day and they were happy about it.

After about two years she said that they sold their house out of town and her husband wanted to move in. I never wanted to rent that bachelor apartment to couples, and had even refused some, because it was so small. *Oh-oh!* What about their dog?

They had a Duck Toller that Hippy-guy would bring with him when he came to visit. The dog didn't seem too friendly to me on the two or three times I saw it. One of the lease conditions was "no dogs allowed", but Hippy-chick assured me that he was a friendly dog. Since she was such a good tenant, I agreed to let hubby and the dog move in. She already had one of the fattest cats I had ever seen, so I figured that was going to be a real zoo. Add on top of that all the puffing they were doing, with all four of them high as kites, I can't imagine how that was going to work out. Or maybe that was the only way to make it work, what did I know!

It turned out that any time I went over there that dog went crazy. It was absolutely vicious. The tenant in the upper one-bedroom loved animals but was terrified of that dog. It only nipped him a couple of times but never bit anyone else that I knew of, only because it was always in the apartment or hooked to a short chain on the deck.

The Hippies were there for another year or so. When it came to the move-out inspection, I found that the carpet was all in shreds. Her fat cat had ripped it to pieces. Hippie-chick said that it was already damaged, so she wasn't responsible for it. I told her she had been a good tenant, and that I had been a good landlord. I gave her the form to sign that forfeited her damage deposit to cover the ruined carpet (which it wouldn't), and she signed it.

*Adios amigos*, and happy toking!

# PART 3
# MUSCLE-UP THAT EQUITY

# CHAPTER 1

# Dutchie's Place

The Triplex was performing well financially. Monthly rents were consistent enough with the two-bedroom and one-bedroom units stable and the bachelor apartment providing about 75% of its potential. Overall, it was performing at over 90%. The banks, at that time, would lend money for mortgages based on 85% of full rents. So, what that meant was if the total rents were, for instance, $1000/month, they would consider the actual income from the property to be $850/month. They would use that figure, along with your personal income, to determine if you exceeded the maximum allowable 30% payment-to-income ratio. Things were looking good financially: the housing market was up, the debt had decreased, and the level of equity was up.

I heard about an over/under duplex that was going to come on the market. It didn't scream out LOCATION LOCATION LOCATION like the Triplex. The street it was on was just so-so and the general area was a bit rough, but it was a solid building and the price, if not fantastic, was very good. The building was vacant and the previous income & expense numbers were very good.

Just like before, I offered the asking price before it was listed on the market. When I received the bank approval, I closed the deal.

The building needed some upgrades and repairs but nothing as extensive as the Triplex. Here I go again!

The roof, electrical, and plumbing were generally good. It formerly was a single-family home that had been converted into an up & down duplex. That meant that the living spaces were fairly small. The lower unit had two small bedrooms, a decent living room with hardwood floors and a fireplace, and a small kitchen and bathroom. It also had a large, southwest facing sunporch. Unfortunately, there was a huge tree out front that must have been about a hundred years old that blocked the sun.

The upper apartment had a similar set up as the lower unit, except a little smaller headroom because of the sloping roofline.

There was a large common porch at the back on the ground level that included the main entrance to the upper apartment, and a washing machine and clothes dryer for the tenants use.

I didn't need a contractor for the renovations for this building, but I did need someone to help me. I was busy enough working my day job, which included a fair amount of travel, along with the regular maintenance and shenanigans at Johnny's.

## "The Grinch"

I had done a lot of renovations to my own home and was pretty handy with the tools. I had rewired the upstairs of the house, installed the plumbing for a washing machine, removed a two-storey chimney, and re-shingled the cedar shingles on the front and one side of the house (that side of the house was 20ft high and about 50ft wide), just to name the more significant projects. When I was going to shingle the other side of the house, I wanted some help, so I mentioned that when I was chatting with my dentist's receptionist. She said her son was a tools guy, too, and was looking for work. I called Grinch and he agreed to come over and help.

Grinch was a former military guy, big and tough at about 6' 1" and 210lbs. He was a good worker and knew what he was doing, but he had this hard edge to him. It took us about ten days to do the job, so we had lots of time to talk. He didn't have much sympathy for people who were "bleeding the system" and he seemed kind of angry all the time.

I could only take so much of his vitriol. I found he would get very agitated when I finally decided to make my beliefs known. We were polar opposites on how we saw things, anything from social security to capital punishment. We covered it all. Towards the end he started opening up about what was bothering him. He said he had gotten divorced and his father had died, both of which he hadn't come to terms with, and he thought he was suffering from depression. He couldn't accept that, because he was raised to "pull himself up by his bootstraps". By the time we finished I could understand where he was coming from, and he seemed more like the rest of us - human.

Back to Dutchie's. I knew Grinch was a good worker and could put his hand to just about anything. I called him to see if he could refinish the hardwood floors and he said he could. He seemed to be more relaxed and joking around this time, almost like his heart had grown three sizes since I'd last seen him. I mentioned this to him, and he said he was feeling better. He told me he had seen his doctor and was on some kind of medication. I remember thinking to myself, *Aha*, trying to look strong and tough all the time when sometimes it's better to just be yourself.

He did a great job on the flooring and I even gave him a fairly good bonus for doing a few other little things that I never asked him to do. *Muy bien!*

## CHAPTER 2

# The Loft


**"G. I. Joe"**

The first tenant in the upper unit was a recently divorced 40-year-old persnickety kind of guy who had his two young sons with him every other weekend. A real spit & polish military trainer who I could never seem to avoid when I went to the gym. "G. I. Joe" was a real power pack – about 5' 7" tall (if that) and about 175lbs. He had what I'd call a thick body and was probably a real muscleman in his younger days. He'd since gone soft and fleshy, but you wouldn't call him fat.

He was one of those guys who seemed to go to the gym sporadically and mostly stand around telling people that he approached at the machines about his past glories. You'd get the sense that this guy could achieve anything since he never had a problem extolling his outstanding abilities. His jokes and sarcastic wit never really quite hit the spot though. His attempts at humour were peppered with a healthy dose of self-deprecation too, which was odd, but the way it was delivered made me think he was just trying to convince people that he was normal. Maybe he was looking for a friend by going there, because he never seemed to have any problem meeting people. To me he came across as a bit arrogant or superior and definitely a tough-as-nails kind of guy. Secretly I thought he might be gay. If I was talking to him and we were anywhere near a flat surface, he would always swipe his fingertips across it and then inspect them to see if there were any offending dust particles on it.

He never caused too many problems other than the minor complaints that would normally crop up with any tenant. One constant complaint with him was the calls about the access to the laundry facilities. *No comprende, Señor!*

That problem comes next.

# CHAPTER 3

# The Den

**"The Entrepreneur"**

She rented out the lower apartment and was in her mid-20s on social assistance with two small children. The rent was paid direct from Social Services, so I never had any problem with that, it was always in-full and on-time. Both bedrooms were very small, along with the rest of the apartment but, somehow, she worked it out for the three of them. She was trying hard enough with upgrading her education so she could find employment. The plumbing and electrical systems were set up so that the landlord meter took care of the common area facilities. This included the outside lighting, the oil-fired boiler, the washing machine, and the clothes dryer.

What I learned from purchasing the first rental property was that I'd be there fixing little things that were missed, probably for the first 4-6 months, so I would be around a fair amount. Plus, I'd be there mowing the lawn or shovelling snow at times too. After a few months I noticed that there seemed to be a lot of laundry either in the machines, or piled up waiting to be washed, or piled on top waiting to be folded and put away. Then came the water and power bills! WOW, what's going on there? Oh right, she has two little kids. That's what all the laundry is about. But wait now, I have two little kids and my water and power bills are not that high.

One day in the gym I talked to G. I. Joe and asked him if things at the apartment were good. He said things were fine, but he'd seen different people coming and going with big black garbage bags quite often. Well, if it wasn't drugs in the bags then what could it be? It turned out that she was *taking in laundry from her friends*, cutting them a deal on the cost (discounted from the price of the laundromat) and pocketing the cash.

Now it's back to the Regulations! The way it works is that if you withdraw a service from a tenant, then that is considered to be equivalent to a rent increase, so it seemed like she couldn't be prevented from using the facilities, however much she wanted. There was no proof that she was abusing or taking advantage of the situation, so what could I do? Hold on a minute! The lease agreement said that laundry facilities were provided, but it didn't say they were free. I went out and bought a coin-operated washing machine and clothes dryer. There was some grumbling, mostly from G. I. Joe, but the calls from him tailed off soon after he realized he could do his laundry when he wanted and that the back porch wasn't a pigsty with dirty laundry (that's one thing he couldn't stand – anything being untidy). Remember, that porch was the main entrance to his apartment.

The Entrepreneur hung in there for a few years and I never really had any serious issues with her. But it's always on move-out day *when you see how people live.* The garbage that came out of there was astounding. I put out thirty-six over-sized garbage bags on the street, plus loose junk comprised of broken toys and stuff that wouldn't fit in bags. I didn't think that the garbage collectors would take it all, but thankfully they did!

# PART 4
# DESCENT INTO MADNESS

**CHAPTER 1**

# Rosie's Place

The building screamed out anything but LOCATION, LOCATION, LOCATION. More like PRICE, PRICE, PRICE.

Johnny's Place and Dutchie's Place were doing pretty well. Except for the situation at the bachelor apartment, all the tenants were paying their rents on time. There was room to expand, buy another property. I was searching around on the internet and eventually came across one I wanted to look at. The price was very low, and it looked like a solid building so I got an agent to show it to me.

It was a purpose-built three-unit building. It had a one-bedroom unit on the basement level with two three-bedroom units above. There was a laundry room in the basement with coin-operated machines. BONUS - $100 extra income a month, or so I thought! The building was in good condition with hardwood floors and Douglas fir trim and interior doors. It looked like it didn't need much for repairs or renovations. It certainly showed well. The three-bedroom units were occupied, and the one-bedroom unit was vacant.

The neighbourhood was, shall I say, less than ideal. On one side there was a 12-unit three-storey walk-up apartment building that didn't look so great, and beside that was a bottle exchange depot. On the other side were two apartment buildings identical to the one I was looking at, but different colours. It's funny how things are in Dartmouth. There can be a perfectly fine residential area and one or two streets away it can go seriously downhill. This was one of those streets.

I decided to dismiss the rule about LOCATION, LOCATION, LOCATION, and go for it.

I did want to put up a fence on either side, especially on the 12-unit building side. There already was one along the back. Who ya gonna call? – "The Grinch", my buddy who had previously helped with the cedar shingling and floor refinishing. He was available to build the fence himself, as by now I just didn't have the time to do it. We went over to the property and I told him how I wanted it built. It was very straight-forward. Auger the holes, set and plumb the 4x4 treated fence posts, pour the cement with the posts *right down in the cement*. Make 8' sections with treated-lumber 2x4 supports for the 4" treated-lumber vertical fence boards. There you go – Bob's your uncle, as we say.

I ordered all the material to have it delivered to the property. In the meantime, I had Grinch pickup an auger I rented over the phone. We measured things out, marked the fence-line and then I left the site. I got a call from Grinch a couple of hours later. He was having some trouble with the auger. He said it was so powerful that he needed a hand controlling it. I had never used an auger before, so he showed me how it worked. There was a horizontal handle on either side at the top with a variable-speed power controller on one of them. Seemed pretty simple, at the time!

Grinch was going to take the controller handle and I would take the other side. I was surprised how heavy the auger was when we picked it up to move it, and Grinch already had a couple of holes drilled all by himself! We got it in place for the next hole and he turned it on. He started it up on slow speed and it seemed to be going okay. Wanting to get the job done quicker, of course, he told me he was going to turn the speed up, and I nodded to him. When it got up to full-speed I knew why he had called me, it was extremely hard to control.

We were struggling mightily to get it under control and all of a sudden it fetched up on something. I don't know what the RPMs on the auger were at that moment, but the blade stopped turning. Something had to give. It really sucks when you don't even have time to say, "Oh S**t!" All the torque got transferred to the upper part of the auger. Before Grinch could let go of the throttle, we both went flying. When that happened, I must have been going about three times faster than a ride on "The Scrambler". I somehow slammed into Grinch. Later I found my glasses about ten feet away in the grass. We looked in the hole and there was a great big boulder that the auger got jammed on. We decided that the job was going to take awhile, so after that fiasco we kept the auger at a slower speed.

That took most of the day and I left Grinch to finish off the fence on his own. I got home and later that night I was really beat, but my right shoulder was really sore. I didn't think much more about it and conked out in bed.

At that time, I was curling once a week. I went to the rink, as usual, the next Saturday morning, and a few hours after I got home my shoulder was bothering me again. This went on for a few weeks. At times there was so much pain that I thought my arm was going to fall off. I knew by now that I had to do something about it, so I went to the doctor. She checked it out and said I had tendinitis, so I started therapy and had to stop curling. After a few weeks I was recovering, somewhat, and decided to go back to the rink again. At one point in the game I had a double take-out to make so on the backswing I raised the rock up pretty high to get up some good momentum for the throw. When I started to bring the rock forward, I felt a severe pain in my shoulder, and I fell to the ice. All the guys came over and asked me what happened. I wasn't in pain anymore, so I told them I didn't know but wanted to go to the changing room. When I took my sweater and shirt off, I thought – OMG, what the hell is that? My bicep muscle looked like it was in a big ball in the crook of my elbow. JEEEZUZ!

I went to the doctor to get it checked out. When I took my shirt off, she said – "OMG, what the hell is that"? Now, far be it from me to give a medical professional advice, but believe me, that's the last thing you want to hear from your doctor! She decided to send me for an x-ray.

Getting older sucks. You start finding out all the intricacies of how the body is constructed and the particulars of why it's not working right. The doctor told me that the reason they call it a bicep is because, of course, there are two muscles there. Each is attached to a tendon, which are attached to the shoulder bone. It turned out that the tendon for the upper muscle let go of the bone, and the muscle slumped down. I went to a specialist and he said I had only lost about 20% of my strength in that arm (apparently, for some reason, those two muscles don't work on a 50/50 basis). He said they don't do surgery to reattach a tendon *on a fifty-year old*. Surgery on a shoulder is too complicated and risky, so I'd have to live with it. Oh, great - it looked ridiculous. At a visit to my own doctor a couple of years later I mentioned that the muscle was coming back to more like normal. When she looked at it, she said that the tendon must have reattached itself, but at a bit lower level because the upper muscle was a little lower down than normal. Good Lord, what next!

Back to the fence. Grinch called a week later and said the fence repair was finished. I went over to see it and it looked great. On closer inspection I noticed that he didn't build it quite the way I had told him. Instead of putting the fence posts directly in the holes *with the cement poured around them,* he had inserted metal spikes in the cement. The spikes are designed to basically place or pound into the ground and have a feature at the top to bolt in a 4x4 fence post. I knew they were okay for a low fence because I had used them before but I didn't like them. I found that the fence was a bit wobbly. This new fence was 6' high, so I asked Grinch why he did that. He said he went out and bought them because he thought that was a better way to build it, but he wouldn't charge me for the spikes. Oh, thanks a lot!

I was concerned enough about using the spikes, but another concern I had was that there was about six inches of the spikes sticking out of the cement. I was worried about what that would mean for the stability of the fence, and rightly so!

One night a few months later I got a call from one of the tenants who was worried about the fence. By now it was fall so we were getting one of our heavy rainstorms, and it was blowing a gale. I went over and the fence was wobbly alright. It was swaying like an accordion! JEEEZUZ!

I went back to my house and got some tools and materials, but God knows what I was going to be able to do. I had to try something because I didn't want to lose the fence.

I had some 1x2 survey stakes with me, so I hammered one of them into the ground about 4' away from the fence, perpendicular to the fence post. Anytime a gust of wind came up I thought the fence was going to flatten me. I nailed a 2x4 to the survey stake and went to nail it to the fence post. The fence was flapping around, and I had to wait until there was a lull in the wind to nail the 2x4 home, which I did. By now I was soaked by the cold rain, and the fences on both sides of the yard were flapping around. I figured a risk assessment was in order. Getting that one brace nailed on took me over half an hour, and there were twelve posts in all for both fences. The risk/reward ratio wasn't looking too good. At least six more hours of work left and probably 4-6 hours in the emergency department at the hospital! All because of those GD metal fence spikes – LORD THUNDERIN' J!

I packed up my tools and materials and took off, happy that I wasn't going to be spending the night in the emergency department. I called Grinch the next day and told him what had happened. We met at the property the next weekend and he apologized. He said he would install the braces no charge as long as I provided the materials. Too bad the fence ended up looking so stupid, but it's the first time I ever thought – who cares, it's a GD rental. *That* was brutal.

# CHAPTER 2

# The Penthouse Suite

**"The Happy Hooker"**

One of the tenants I inherited from the previous owner was a woman in her late-20s. She had three young children. They were in the top apartment and were the only ones listed on the lease as living there. I soon received the expected nuisance calls to fix this, that, and the other thing. After a few calls from her (plugged drains, leaking taps, and so on), I noticed that a guy seemed to be there all the time. I asked her if he was living there and she said he was living with his mother but stayed overnight with her a couple of times a week to be with his daughter. Apparently, he was the father of her youngest daughter. This guy was a real tall drink of water, about 6'4" and 240lbs. He worked construction - they probably used him as a crane!

When the heavy rains came in the fall, I was over there quite a bit. There was (here we go again) a sump hole in the laundry room. This was a much more modern building than Johnny's Place, with a poured cement foundation, so I couldn't imagine why it was put in. Regardless, there was some minor flooding at times that I always had to keep an eye on.

Many times, I was over there later in the evening dealing with the laundry room or fixing something at her place. This would be like 9pm or later, and she'd be dressed to the nine's, full make-up, red lipstick, high heels, hair all done up. "Hmm, wonder where she's going dressed like that at this time of night?"

She started shorting me out on the rent right away, always going to get the rest to me next week, which never came. So, she's on welfare, getting the childcare payments, hooking at night, and the boyfriend is working under the table and looking after the kids at night. Right, can't afford the rent. Seemed like a pretty sweet set-up to me. Well, money-wise. Perhaps not otherwise.

I decided to give her notice to vacate by registered mail. She called me to come over a few days later to fix something. Yeah, right – more like to fix me. Crane-man was there when I arrived. He started going on about me being too chickenshit to give her notice in person. I still can't believe I did this, but by now I'd had it with the ridiculous situations I was finding myself in. I told him he wasn't on the lease, so it wasn't any of his business. Of course there had to be a consequence to that statement - on my way out after a brief chat with the Hooker, he came out in the hall and whispered to me that I'd better sleep with one eye open at night.

On my way home I was thinking about what he said. I called the police and two officers arrived at my house. The female officer came in and I told her what happened and that the guy threatened me. She said that a general comment like that is not considered by the courts to be a "threat", it was just a "warning". WTF! She said that to be considered a threat, it has to be specific, like – "I'm going to stab you" or "I'm going to break your legs". Good Lord, I thought, what has this world come to?

The officer asked if I had the Hooker's number, which I did. She gave her a call to talk it over. When the officer mentioned that the boyfriend had threatened me, I could hear the Hooker yell out asking her boyfriend, (calling to him by name), if he'd threatened me. Apparently, the officer was familiar with the Hooker's domestic and professional life, because she said, "Hold on – is he there now"? Obviously, he was. The officer reminded the Hooker that she had a restraining order against him. OMG, this is insane. She had quite a long conversation with the Hooker and made it clear that there better not be anymore "warnings" to the landlord, and she better move out at the end of the month.

I think I dodged a bullet there, literally. She paid her back-rent and moved out as scheduled. She even asked me for a reference for her next victim, er, landlord.

## "Popeye & Olive Oil"

BATTER-UP! The next one along to move into the top unit was a grandmother who had custody of her three grandchildren, again on social assistance. The rent was paid direct to my account. *Perfect*, or so I thought.

After she moved in, I soon found out that her partner was living with them. He was a retired Coast Guard officer. Hmm, nice fat pension, I imagined. With that and the social services payments, plus the childcare money, they should be able to make a go of it.

It seems everybody needs to tell you their sob stories, even so much as showing off their physical scars (which definitely should remain hidden). I can't count the number of hernia, appendix, and various other scars from operations I've seen. Now that I think of it, I've seen more dental abscesses than I could shake a stick at. Thankfully no one's gone so far as to show me a vasectomy scar!

It came to pass that, unfortunately, Olive Oil had cancer. Sure enough, she'd had an operation. At least she had the decency *to ask* if I wanted to see the scar. I delightfully declined the invitation!

She was struggling taking care of the three grandkids, but Popeye seemed to be a big help. At this point I couldn't care less who was staying where or who was listed on the lease, as long as the rents were being paid.

## CHAPTER 3

# Between a Rock & a Hard Place

**"Mother Mary"**

Mary was in the middle unit when I bought the building and she worked a couple of part-time jobs, one of them at a Catholic bookstore. She lived below the Happy Hooker when I bought the building. She called me plenty of times, not as much for repair jobs, but more for the shenanigans going on upstairs. I could tell she was trying her best to be a do-gooder and to convert the Hooker, without much success. She was worried about Crane-man's behaviour and how he was treating his girlfriend. I told her I wasn't going to get involved in that. At one point they had some kind of altercation because when I next saw her, she had a black eye. She said she was trying to help the Hooker and I guess she stuck her nose in the wrong place. She said she never called the police because Crane-man "warned" her not to.

Mary eventually got back on her rent and she moved out without giving notice. I couldn't find out where she moved to, so I went to the bookstore where she worked. She was there so I gave her notification of the hearing at the Tenant board, right in front of some customers. She said that "wasn't very considerate of me". HA! I went to the hearing, but she didn't show up. The adjudicator eventually ruled in my favour for back-rent plus one-month's rent for vacating without giving notice. A fat lot of good that did me, she had quit her job at the bookstore, and I had no idea where she was living. *Madre Maria!*

## "The Cable Gals"

After the Happy Hooker and Mother Mary moved out, two women, both with kids, occupied the two 3-bedroom units. Both were on social assistance. The one in the middle unit never caused me too much grief other than the amount of garbage she seemed to generate. After the previous two tenants had moved out, the garbage bin seemed to be much fuller every week.

*Cable Gal 1*, who moved into the top unit, couldn't get the power company to hook her up (because of a previous non-payment problem) so she asked if I could *include it in the rent*. HOLD ON! I've been down that road before. There was no way that was going to happen, which really pissed her off. I went over a couple of days later to see what was going on. The front windows of the top and middle units were open a bit and there was an extension cord and a cable TV wire running between the two apartments. I went up to find out what that was all about. It turned out that the one in the middle couldn't get cable TV service so the one in the top was sending it down to her from a splitter in her apartment. In exchange, the one in the middle was sending power to the one in the top for her fridge, a couple of lights, and her TV…JEEEZUZ!

It was becoming apparent that these people on social services had some kind of social network. They seemed to know all about each other's business, and some were on friendly terms and some weren't. There wasn't much I could do, but I couldn't imagine *Cable Gal 1* carrying on like that for too long. Naturally, it didn't. She moved out after a few days and didn't give me notice. No Tenant Board hearing this time, why bother?

When she moved in, she had given me six months of post-dated cheques. I tried to cash the next one, but it came back "Insufficient Funds". I went to her bank, which was the same one as mine, and talked to the teller about the situation. She said the bank could put the cheque in the system to be cashed as soon as enough money appeared in the account. There was a small charge for the service, so I got her to do it. A couple of weeks later the cheque cleared and the money went into my account. *Yahoo*!

The next day I got a call from her father. He was enraged. He said I didn't have any right to cash that cheque, so I told him to apply to the Tenant Board to get it back, *Ethel*!

*Cable Gal 2* in the middle unit had a young daughter who was maybe 17-years-old or so. One day I was doing some repairs in the laundry room, which was directly below one of the bedrooms in the middle unit. It was the middle of the afternoon and I heard two people above me in the throes of passion. After what seemed like a long time it stopped, and I heard them talking. Oh right, only the young ones can go at it like that! It was the daughter and her boyfriend. After a few months I never saw the boyfriend around again, and a few months after that I could tell she had a bun in the oven. Alas, the cycle continues.

## CHAPTER 4

# Six Feet Under

**"Quasimodo"**

The basement apartment was vacant at the time I bought the building. I got a new tenant for the unit, a guy in his mid-30s. The poor guy had a hunchback and seemed like he was a few bricks shy of a load, but he was working, and *seemed like a nice guy – at the time.*

It was raining hard the day he was going to move in and I got a call from him in the morning. He was at the apartment and had moved a few things in, just stuff he could get in his car. When he had returned to the apartment with more stuff, the place was flooded. It was just enough water to cover the hardwood floors. Obviously, he couldn't move in until I got that sorted out, but since he was moving in a few days early he could still stay at his other apartment. Back I went to farting around with pumps and water problems!

I got everything fixed up and he moved in. The next Spring, I noticed his car was up on blocks in the driveway. The area wasn't great looking to begin with, but that certainly didn't help. I asked him what was wrong with the car and how long it would be until he got it repaired. He said there was a problem with the gas tank, and he was looking for another one. I asked him if he could try to get it fixed asap because it didn't look too good sitting there up on blocks. He said he'd try to get it done by the next weekend.

When I went over to the side door of the building the next Saturday, his car was still up on blocks and I noticed a big black plastic garbage can on the deck. It smelled pretty strong – HOLD ON! That's gasoline in there. It was more than half-full, sitting there with no top, not in an approved container. OMG! Forget the Regulations, what kind of moron would do that. The tenants on the upper floors regularly threw their cigarette butts out the windows above. I knew because I'd see them do it, and the resulting mess on the driveway below. Good God, what do you do with that?

I told him clearly, so there was absolutely no room for confusion, to get the bucket of gasoline *off the property immediately*, or I would. I had no idea at that point what I would do with it. I left and went home, but of course couldn't stop thinking about it. I decided I needed some advice, so I called the police and asked them if it was illegal to store an open bucket of gas that way. The officer didn't know but asked me to hold on the line. When she came back, she said she asked around and everyone thought it wasn't illegal – but they all agreed that it was pretty stupid! She transferred me over to the fire department. I explained the situation to them, and they said they'd send someone around to check it out.

A couple of hours later I went over to see what had transpired. He was there and the bucket of gas was still there on the deck. He started giving me grief about sending the fire department over. I was beside myself. I needed to get that gasoline away from the building. I wondered what I could do with it. I didn't have any approved containers. It looked like I'd need a few of them because it looked like a lot of gas. This was crazy, maybe I could get the water hose out, pour the gas on the back lawn, light it on fire…wait, OMG, I'm starting to think like these people! I needed to lay it on the line with him in a one-way conversation.

After I emphatically, and with no small amount of animation, told Quasimodo to get the open bucket of gasoline off the side deck of the apartment building, I could see the gears slowly start to turn in his head, searching for a way to save his precious fuel. When his moment of Eureka finally arrived, he grabbed the bucket, struggled to take it down the stairs and over to his broken-down car…..and proceeded to put it on the back seat!

I thought, fine. I'll come back later, put a match to it, and have the car and building go up in smoke. By this time, I was really starting to lose it. Ahhh, *Livin' La Vida Loca!*

### "Two-Bills Annie"

Another younger woman and her boyfriend moved into the basement apartment after Quasimodo moved out. They both looked like they'd been around the block, more than once. They were both working and their finances, if not references, were good.

Shortly after, Olive Oil said to me "watch out for her, she's a nasty one". Well, what the hell did she mean by that? When I asked her, she said that she knew her from another building she lived in and there was always trouble. I could tell, as Jed Clampett would have put it, "they were going to get along as good as two dogs with one bone". None of my business, or so I thought.

Some kind of dispute erupted between the two of them later on. I got a call from Olive Oil one night and she said that I should come over because the police were there. I didn't want to get involved because at the time I was having a beer with my neighbour. He asked me what was going on and, always being one for adventure, he suggested we go over. I agreed to go but told him to just stay in the car when we got there. By the time we arrived the police had left. Annie and Olive Oil were taking turns coming out to me in the front and carrying on with some gibberish about who did what to whom. Popeye appeared at one point shaking his head. I look at him, rubbed my chin, and said to him, "If anybody gets stabbed – call the police"!

My buddy just laughed, and we took off for home to have a few more beers!

A few months later Annie reminded me of a trick a guy showed me when I was living out west. She always paid me in cash, which I would get when I went to collect the rents at the building. One night on the first of the month she appeared at my kitchen door and said she had the rent. That had never happened before, and her behaviour seemed kind of strange. She looked nervous and she quickly walked over to the kitchen counter. She had a stack of bills, all 20's, and each one was folded in half. She proceeded to put each one down on the counter, one on top of the other, while counting them out. She left right away before I could write out her receipt. I never thought much about it until I unfolded the bills to check the count. That's something I always did in front of the tenant's who paid cash. OH HO! One of the bills was cut in half, so instead of having thirty $20 bills I really had 28 plus two halves (at least the serial numbers matched!).

I thought, you shyster (or words to that effect). Then I thought - she has no proof that she gave me any money because, in her haste to escape from the scene of the crime, she forgot to get her receipt. Ha-ha, gotcha!

I immediately went over to her apartment. She looked even more nervous than before and tried to play coy about it at first. I told her that I hadn't seen that trick in a long time. She tried to put on a look of horror as if she would never do something like that. The conversation got a little heated. She finally told me she didn't care and there was nothing I could do about it anyway. I said fine, let me see your receipt for the rent payment. OOPS! She knew I couldn't prove she shorted me out, but she couldn't prove that she had paid the rent. That's when she decided to give me the other twenty dollars. *Muchas gracias, Ethel*!

# PART 5
# TRUTHS & CONSEQUENCES

There were several things I learned during my time as a landlord which I wish I had thought about before I went down this road. That's not to say I still wouldn't have done it, but I would have had a better understanding of what was ahead. Some of those things are related to the way people are and the way they behave, and some are related to maintaining the investments. It seems to me that both had their own consistent aspects, and they probably ring true for most landlords.

## Maintenance & Repairs

There was a whole pile of work to do, all the time, with eight apartments in three buildings. Lawns to mow, trees and shrubs to trim, driveways to shovel, garbage to take out, minor electrical repairs, taps and faucets to fix.

About 90% of the repair issues in the buildings were related to water. Mold problems, damaged gyproc, odd toilet models and fitting sizes that some previous nut-job landlord had installed that I couldn't find matching pieces for. I know from doing extensive repairs in my own 100-year old house that sometimes you need to be innovative, but that doesn't mean buying stuff at flea markets and trying to make it work or fit on a repair job. I still can't believe the number of times I stewed for days over why somebody had done something like that, and the grief it caused me to tear it out and fix it correctly.

As far as the great payoff on the coin operated laundry machines was concerned, forget about it. I spent more money repairing and replacing them than I ever brought in. The tenants would somehow use slugs or find ways to jimmy them, which always led to damage. So much for the hoped for under-the-table fun money.

I always enjoyed doing construction type stuff and had done a lot of it over the years. There was the cedar shingling, lots of plumbing & electrical jobs, the chimney removal (with a jackhammer), and a nice two-level wrap around deck at my house. The one thing I hated, which I know is really the transformative feature to a space, was painting. I hated it with a passion. First you have to clean the surface, especially if the tenants were smokers, or else the paint won't stick. I don't even want to talk about ceilings! Taping off was tricky for me and seemed to take forever. Try to do it without taping off, that takes forever too and never works out. Then when you get the first coat of paint on…YOU HAVE TO DO IT ALL AGAIN!

If I spent 90% of my repair time working on water problems, I spent 90% of my tenant move-out time painting. One tenant at Rosie's place had asked if she could paint the living room. I said sure, as long as it wasn't black! When she moved out, it was time to get out the sandpaper. It seemed her hand-to-eye coordination left something to be desired, or maybe she'd been into the sauce before she started the job. She had run the roller up onto the Douglas fir trim and baseboards in lots of places. I couldn't leave it like that, it looked horrendous.

## Garbage & Cleaning

Let me talk about garbage for a minute – OOOHHH, don't get me started on that! How in the world do people on limited incomes generate *so much garbage*? Sure, I sort and separate my garbage and try not to generate too much waste, and it doesn't take much time or effort. Rosie's had a well constructed wooden garbage bin that was about 12' x 3' x 4' for the three apartments. When I bought the building, it was over-full. I had to clean it out – NO WAIT! I had to set it on fire! It was absolutely disgusting, full of bags of rotting food and maggots. And the stench, OMG - make you want to cry out for your mother!

The garbage pick-up was every 2 weeks in the neighbourhood, and I'd go over every two weeks to put it out, rain, shine, sleet, or snow. I had to because the tenants wouldn't take it out and there was so much of it. The bin could have been full, but it was usually half full because the other half was laying on the lawn or driveway beside it. One day I saw a bag of garbage come flying out of the kitchen window in the top unit. Every garbage day there were no less than 22 black bags – FOR 3 APARTMENTS! I was able to reduce it to that by stuffing several of the smaller kitchen-type bags they'd thrown out into the black bags I brought with me. Real bonus there though – I got to claim the cost of the bags as an expense – *Yahoo*! After the first month I got to claim another related expense. The birds, feral cats, and rats were having meals fit for a king, ripping into the bags. Loose garbage ended up all over the sidewalk. I bought cans of Lysol spray and sprayed the outside of the bags after I set them out. That worked when it wasn't raining. On rainy days I had to adjust my defenses and spray inside the bags too. I was starting to feel like Winston

Churchill, an accomplished master of defense. Okay, hold on here. You're really losing it now buddy!

Move-out days were usually eye-popping experiences. Like I said before, that's when you see how people live. It got to the point where I could assess in a few minutes how many hours of work it would take me to get a place ready to show. The fridge and stove almost always needed cleaning. I probably could've fed an army with the amount of food I removed from fridges and cupboards, and that was just the stuff that was edible. The science projects were another story! I felt terrible about simply throwing it out without separating the compostables, and actually worried at times that the garbage collectors would realize what was in the bags and refuse to take it.

At home I'd rinse out things like glass jars, plastic bags, and anything that had contained food, and then separate them for recycling. I wouldn't dare touch some of the stuff I came across in the apartments and just chucked it in the regular garbage bags, sprayed with Lysol of course!

I had been worried about Tex dropping a cigarette and burning down Johnny's Place. *Ha*! I realized that that was the least of my worries when he moved out. There were hundreds of plastic and paper garbage bags jammed in behind his fridge which could have heated up and started a fire.

## Christmas

I knew what was coming if a tenant got back on their rent in October or November. They were headed for trouble, and so was I! Christmas was on the way, and they had no trouble establishing their priorities - their "Christmas Lists" - and paying the rent wasn't one of the items. Sure enough, without fail, they'd "default". Then they would be apologetic and promise to get it sorted out in January. *Ha!* Remember, it was the season of giving. Yeah, the season of giving eviction notices! The problem was that they weren't just overdue on their rent. They would be overdue on their power bills, cable bills, phone bills, and credit card bills. They'd get into this spiral of debt that they had no hope of getting out of. They'd then go out to a money lender with exorbitant interest rates to keep the creditors at bay. The trouble is, they'd never borrow enough money TO PAY THE RENT! Why was the landlord always forgotten? Oh right, he can go the Tenant Board. *Feliz Navidad!*

## The Tenancy Board

I get it, tenants need protection, no problem there. I know there are plenty of landlords who treat their tenants like dirt. They don't fix or repair things and sometimes do things that are way over the line. It takes two to tango though. Lots of tenants don't pay their rent and do the most outrageous things you can imagine. There needs to be an intermediary to resolve these disputes, and in its infinite wisdom the government created the Tenant Board. I'm a real process kind of guy. I think that clear, written procedures are important so that everybody knows how things work and what to expect. At the same time, that can be a bad thing.

**"Pacific Heights"** – Well, it didn't go *that* far, but one tenant I had knew the procedures through-and-through. He got back on his rent a bit, but he wasn't delinquent in full. The next month he made up his back-rent but paid nothing toward the current month. The regulations state that I could give him an eviction notice, but if he paid within 15-days I would have to revoke the notice. Great, so I couldn't advertise the apartment for rent because if he paid within that time he could stay, and I couldn't rent it out to someone else.

As it turned out he didn't pay and didn't move out. I applied for a hearing at the Tenant Board, and got a hearing scheduled for *three weeks later*! I still couldn't advertise it for rent because I didn't know what was going to happen. I was familiar enough with the regulations that I knew it could take awhile, and so did he. He showed up at the hearing and he didn't have a leg to stand on. The adjudicator said he would mail out his decision within two weeks. OK, that takes us in to another month of unpaid rent.

The decision came through on the 6th of the next month. The tenant was ordered to pay the back-rent and move out immediately. By this point our "relationship" was on the rocks. I needed to talk to him to see what he intended to do, because I wanted to advertise the apartment. He wasn't ornery or anything. He just shrugged his shoulders and said he'd do what he had to do, and I could do what I had to do. *What the hell did that mean*?

He knew the system alright, and so did I. The Tenant Board can't enforce an order for payment. That comes from the courts. I had to pay a fee for a Small Claims Court hearing, which was scheduled for the end of the month. He didn't show up for the hearing, so I got an order from the court for eviction and payment of all monies due, including court costs. *Yahoo*! Or so I thought. I sent him his notice by registered mail, which I had tracking on, and he received it a few days later. It didn't seem to faze him in the least. When I went to see him, he said, "Remember what I said before – you do what you need to do". OMG, this guy really knows how to play the system. I had to pay another fee to the Sheriff (which again I could claim back from the tenant, *Ha-ha*) to have him removed from the apartment. That was scheduled for the 21$^{st}$ of the next month.

Living dangerously is not one of my fortes, but I decided to go for it! I advertised the apartment for rent. I told the callers that it wouldn't be ready to show until the 23$^{rd}$ of the month. Most of them wanted to find a place early in the month so they could get out of their current apartment at the end of the month, so that put a squeeze on them, and me. I was already out 3 month's rent and it looked like this situation might make it four.

Well, the tenant moved out before the Sheriff came to give him the boot. You know the expression "one bad decision leads to another". I was all too familiar with it in my golfing days - Try to avoid taking a "drop", then it all goes to s**t. The only prospective tenant that was in a situation to move in that fast was a woman around 30-years old. "The Dealer" moved in but...*she seemed like a nice lady, at the time.*

I owned Rosie's for thirty months, and during that time there were 13 evictions, all for non-payment. You do the math – 3 apartments times 30 months, minus, minus, minus…you get my drift. I never had to follow the whole process through to the Sheriff again, but I had to go through a lot of hurdles at times. The expenses mostly were being paid and there actually was a positive balance more months than not, but there was an awful lot of grief to go with it.

## The Books

On top of all this insanity, the accounting had to be done. All the receipts, invoices, and documents had to be sorted and reconciled with the bank account. Is it only me, but why did the insurance company always send a copy of something they had already sent me a few days before, and sometimes a third copy? It was hard enough to keep everything else straightened out without having to interpret their GD 26-page documents to see if they were identical! Everything needed to be put in the correct envelop for each property. Then came tax time. Thank God for spreadsheets and accountants!

## Debt, Equity & Lifestyle

Wasn't the whole point of this to create wealth and secure a comfortable retirement? As the equity grows and the debt decreases, things start to look like they're moving in the right direction. But wait a minute! You've gotta live a little and enjoy life, right? You've heard all the expressions – "you only live once", "you can't take it with you", "live for today – plan for tomorrow".

I always loved to travel. I had been to places like Britain & Turkey and Alaska & California, and many places in between. I wanted my two young kids to have great vacations during March Break. Get away from it all, put our feet up, and give us some interesting experiences and memories. I was plowing money into RRSPs, RPPs, and RESPs so there wasn't a lot of cash lying around. Hey, maybe I could draw on some of the equity for that.

As a kid I had some great vacations with my parents and siblings going camping and boating. My Mom and Dad worked hard at their jobs and hard at home making sure we had not a good life growing up, but a great life and a lot of fun. Our vacations weren't about flying off to beaches down south. We had them right there on our river every summer! We had the greatest summer vacations, camping and boating and visiting family and friends along the river.

Let me tell you, the only thing you're going to experience on a sandy beach in Nova Scotia in March is frostbite! So, the decision was an easy one – take out some equity. Maybe not the right decision, time will tell. I suppose the question is - if I make it to eighty-five, do I want to be counting coins and possessions or having great memories & eating hot dogs and Kraft Dinner? I'll take the latter, *muchas gracias!*

We took the trips, awesome trips, to Costa Rica, Disney/Orlando, Daytona Beach, a cruise to the Bahamas, and then to southern Spain. It sure burnt up some of the equity but was worth every penny, whatever happens from here on in. I know I've been extremely fortunate in life, with two children who I love so much and had so much fun with. What's eventually written in the obituary or on the gravestone will never tell the story, or matter to me, because I'll be 6' under! (but not at Rosie's Place). And maybe as skinny as the Druid.

## The Good, The Bad & The Ugly

Obviously, after all is said and done, I can't say that this rental business was a cakewalk. But what business is? I can neither recommend it, nor dissuade anyone from it. Real Estate is a great place to be, but I'm not sure I'd do it *that way* again! Nor can I say that the people in this story are representative of all tenants. Just like any business there are good and bad customers or clients. I had many tenants who came and went and never caused me any grief at all, and in fact were very helpful at times in one way or another. The tenants who did set my blood to boiling weren't necessarily bad people. They were, I think, just plunged into life with 3-strikes against them from the get-go. I don't believe they set out to not pay their rent or their bills. They themselves probably were shorted out so many times in life, in so many ways, that they just gave up caring. Of the mountain of challenges they faced, not cleaning up their apartment on move-out day or not separating their garbage was probably the least of their concerns.

Let's go back to the risk/reward ratio. When I was a renter out west, I spent countless hours cleaning my apartment coming up to move-out day because I wanted to get my damage deposit back. It was always returned to me, and always in full. When Social Services is paying the tab, they don't come looking for the damage deposit returned, they just pay it again on the client's new place. Given that, what's really to be gained by cleaning up? Sure, a few bucks (because it goes back to the tenant), but one hell of a lot of work to get it!

At some point you just have to accept the reality of the way things are and - Suck it up buttercup and Get 'er done. There was no point in steaming about facing a job that you shouldn't even have to be doing, that just made the job worse. Might as well turn on the tunes and get out...the paint supplies, *Arrgh*!!!

It might seem that my life during this time was an endless and daily series of upheaval and torment, when it really wasn't, or was it? As a landlord, I would be doing something with one of the units on a regular basis, but probably only once every week or two. Sometimes there was even a lull for a month or two. When I was travelling for work or on vacation, I had an electrician and a plumber I could call if anything went wrong. As a parent, I was also taking care of my kids, getting them off to school, taking them to all their music & swimming lessons, and volleyball & soccer activities. Where in the world do you get the time and energy for that? Oh right, they were my kids, so that's what you do. Having those experiences and memories were everything. It was priceless to see them doing all that stuff! I wouldn't have missed it for the world, and I never did. So, I guess there *was* a lot of upheaval and turmoil, but there also was a healthy dose of pleasure and fun to go with it. God knows how I had time to have a few beers now and again, but I managed to (but not at Shrek's).

The physical assets (the buildings) were the easier part, even though they could be the biggest drain on time, and to some degree money. But they could be fixed. When something was damaged or broken it was frustrating, and sometimes maddening, but there is no point in yelling at an inanimate object, right! You'd just end up looking like an idiot. A solution could always be found, and it would be over and done with.

The people side (the tenants) was a different kettle of fish! Or was it, really? Sure, there's no solution to someone's upbringing. They thought the way they thought, they saw things the way they saw things, and you'll never understand why they don't get what you're saying. And that will never change. Now that I think about it, they were similar, in a way, to inanimate objects. Yelling at them wasn't going to change anything and again, you'd just end up looking like an idiot. It's like talking to someone who doesn't speak English – speaking louder doesn't make them understand any better what you're saying.

Obviously, buildings can't turn on you like a person can. There's no fear of them drawing a knife on you. However, there are plenty of risks involved with them. With the number of times I was on ladders and roofs, in spaces not meant to be in, working with power tools, and rewiring or replumbing stuff, it would have been easy to get injured. I was fortunate enough to come away unscathed, other than the bicep thing. *Whew!*

Why did it seem that so many times when I had a "disagreement" with a tenant, they were all over 6' tall? Well, that's not quite true, but they're the ones who might have pulled a knife on me. And I wouldn't have been surprised if they had. Again, I was fortunate enough to come away unscathed, other than suffering several brain cramps. *Double Whew!*

# PART 6
# ESCAPE FROM THE ABYSS

So, the whole point of this was to create wealth, eh!

I considered at this point selling all three buildings and using the equity to buy a bigger building, have everything under one roof. Perhaps the *provincial mental institution*! Seriously though, the idea was to leverage debt. If a bank was willing to lend the money, and the income was paying the debt, even if the margin was small, you still get the capital appreciation if you hold the investment long enough. It just so happened during the thirty months of owning Rosie's that the housing market took a spike up. The equity out of the three properties would be enough to put a deposit on a 12 or 16-unit building. I searched the internet and there were a few available. None were in the right price range though. They were either too high a price (meaning in a good area), or too low a price (meaning the opposite). After I reflected a little, I felt I just didn't have it in me anymore.

Timing is everything. It so happened that the company I was working for was downsizing. I had been there for thirteen years. It's nice to be paid well but it can be risky too, especially if you're the top paid employee in your department. It turned out that I "got voted off the island". I was 57-years old…what to do? I re-married around this time and I had been putting money into RRSP and RPP savings. The termination payout was alright, so I decided to analyse the finances. It didn't look too bad, pretty good in fact. I certainly wasn't rich, far from it, but I thought about my father and what happened to him. He was in the Navy in World War 2 and worked hard for over 40 years. Sadly, he died one-and-a-half years into his retirement. He was the greatest guy and greatest father, and never got to enjoy what he deserved for his retirement. He was only 66-years old when he died.

I've often thought I was not a risk-taker by nature, but when I look back perhaps that's not entirely true. I have certainly never been a daredevil, throwing myself out of an airplane to experience the exhilaration of parachuting, or possibly dying. I feel absolutely no compulsion to try and cheat death. I'd prefer that it comes in its own way, rather than seek it out. At the same time, I have taken risks, but they just don't include death as one of the potential outcomes. Well, mostly, thinking now about Crane-man!

When I was twenty-years old I hitch-hiked out to Alberta. After eleven years I left a guaranteed-for-life job there and started a new career 4000 kilometers away when I was thirty-one years old. After eight years there I left that guaranteed-for-life job and took a position as a regional manager of a sales/distribution operation for a national company. After five years there I left that job and worked as a project manager for a somewhat unstable contractor, that eventually was bought out by a large multi-national company. I guess what I'm saying is that I *have* taken risks, mostly well considered risks. My decision to retire at 57-years old was a risk, and not an easy decision to make. I assessed everything: the amount of equity, the amount of savings, the level of expenses, inflation factors, how much fudge-factor there should be, what the markets might do (what a crapshoot that is!).

I decided to take the plunge, but what would I do with my days. I was lucky enough to have been on the

Board of our local food bank for over ten years. At the time of my retirement, I was the vice-president. I started helping out there two days a week. Two years later my turn came up to be president. It was a volunteer position for a three-year term. It was a real hands-on position so that kept me busy a lot, at different times, throughout the week. That was truly the most rewarding experience I'd ever had. I met most of the clients, who easily could have been one of my past tenants, and a couple of them actually were. I can't describe how nice these people were. They were respectful, helpful setting up tables and chairs, and very rarely caused any trouble. We had almost one hundred clients a week who would come in for food, and many of them had their spouses and kids with them. It could easily have turned into mayhem, but never did.

After my term as president was done, my wife Debra and I started to talk about what the rest of our lives might look like. The kids had grown up. We had vacationed for four weeks every year, for the last six years, in a small town in southern Spain. She'd had a successful business for over ten years in Nova Scotia, but we absolutely hated the weather, especially the cold in the winter. I had worked outdoors for almost twenty years of my career and was completely fed up with the rain, drizzle, sleet, freezing rain, *freezing fog*. Good Lord, how many weather terms can they come up with that we faced on a regular basis? Maybe I hit the limit when I heard the latest one – *freezing ice pellets*. What the hell is that? Aren't ice pellets already frozen?

We decided to see if it was feasible for my wife to open a similar business in Spain. We went there for a week and assessed the possibility. The town we always went to was beautiful. It had tons of British and English-speaking European residents and tourists. When we had vacationed there my wife was always asking people about topics related to her business, just natural curiosity. She knew there were a lot of people there who were not satisfied with the service they were getting. We realized that the potential was there. *Next Risk Coming Up!*

We got our documentation in order, sold everything, and made the move. We've been living in our lovely little town on the Mediterranean Sea going on two years now. But, of course, it wasn't quite as simple as that…

# AUTHOR'S NOTES

The situations described in this memoir are as accurate as I can recall. Some details have been omitted, as to include them would have complicated the writing and reading of the story. One of those facts was that I was married during part of that time and my partner had some involvement in the overall picture. That fact, from a practical point of view, had no bearing on the events that I experienced. These are my personal memories, as only I experienced them in a very up-close and personal way.

The timing of certain events in this memoir are not precisely accurate. The progression of purchases and the cast of characters, however, are.

I want to thank several people, first of whom is my wonderful wife, Debra. She is and has always been an incredible source of positivity, reasonableness, and a calming influence for me, even in the face of incredible adversity. And I'm not just referring to tenant situations.

My sister Cindy and friend Denise were extremely helpful with their editing skills, suggesting several improvements to the text, structure, and formatting of the book. Appreciative shout-outs to you both.

I also want to thank my dear mother and father for giving me everything, and more. Our home was such a fun place to be and I could never imagine having a better childhood or growing up anywhere else.

# ABOUT THE AUTHOR

Kevin Clarke grew up along the lower Saint John River in New Brunswick.

The first half of his career was spent working in the telephone industry in Alberta and Nova Scotia in various roles, primarily as a pole-line and underground cabling technician. His other career choices included several years as a regional sales manager for a national distribution company, a project manager for a communications contractor, and a safety specialist for a power and communications conglomerate.

Kevin enjoys helping people, having spent fifteen years on the Board of Directors of his local food bank, three of those as a hands-on manager after he retired.

He likes to travel, swim, read, and listen to music of every genre, particularly flamenco.

He has two daughters and two stepchildren, all adults, and lives with his awesome wife in southern Spain.

www.ingramcontent.com/pod-product-compliance
Lightning Source LLC
LaVergne TN
LVHW041641060526
838200LV00040B/1666